3RD EDITION

7 STEPS TO GROW CANNABIS

A COMPLETE BEGINNER'S GUIDE TO GROWING CANNABIS INDOORS

BY MR GROW IT

7 Steps To Grow Cannabis: A Complete Beginner's Guide
To Growing Cannabis Indoors, 3rd Edition
Copyright © 2020 by Mr. Grow It

ISBN: 978-1-7351961-0-7

Cover photo: @phenofocus

Principle photography © Mr. Grow It

Additional photography by: @northwest.jay, @nugs.jpg, @liftedmacro, @mr.canucksgrow, @phenofocus, growweedeasy.com, @veedubgrow

All rights reserved. No part of this book may be reproduced, distributed, or transmitted in any form or by any means, including photocopying, recording, or other electronic or mechanical methods, without the prior written permission of the author, except in the case of brief quotations embodied in critical reviews and certain other noncommercial uses permitted by copyright law. For permission requests, email the author, addressed "Attention: Permission Request", at the address below.

contact@mrgrowit.com

Visit www.MrGrowIt.com

DISCLAIMER:

This book is meant to provide information about growing cannabis. The content in this book is for educational purposes only. The legal aspects of growing cannabis vary in different countries. Hence, readers are advised to use their own discretion and abide by the laws of their country for growing cannabis. The author does not advocate breaking the law. The use of any information provided in this book is solely at your own risk. Although every precaution has been taken to verify the accuracy of the information contained herein, the author assumes no responsibility for any errors or omissions. No liability is assumed for damages that may result from the use of information contained within.

To the 10 million people who have watched my cannabis grow videos over the past 5 years and the 100,000+ followers on social media who support me. This is for you.

Thank you!

What's INSIDE THIS BOOK?

01

Introduction VI
Equipment

Grow Tent	4
Lighting	7
Ventilation System	14
Oscillating Fan	17
Grow Pot	18
Growing Medium & Nutrients	22
Humidifier, Dehumidifier, Heater, Air Conditioner	25
Setting Up The Equipment	28

02

Seeds

Getting Seeds	34
Bag Seeds	37
Types of Seeds	38
Germinating Seeds	40
Planting Seeds	43

03

Environment

Temperature	50
Humidity	52
Air Circulation	59
CO_2	55
Balancing Temperature & Humidity	57

04

Vegetation

Light Cycle & Distance	60
Watering	62
pH	65
PPM	68
Feeding Nutrients	70
Weeks 1-2	75
Weeks 3+	77
Transplanting	79
Low-Stress Training (LST)	82
Topping	85
Pruning	86

06

Harvest

Harvesting	102
Trimming	105
Drying	109
Curing	111

Epilogue   130
Glossary   131

05

Flower

Forcing Flowering	90
Sexing	91
Weeks 1-3	93
Weeks 4+	95
Flushing	98

07

Problems

pH Fluctuations	117
Heat Stress & Light Burn	118
Over-Watering & Under-Watering	120
Nitrogen Deficiency	121
Nitrogen Toxicity	122
Calcium Deficiency	123
Fungus Gnats	124
Bud Rot & Mold	125
Nutrient Burn	126
Hermies & Bananas	127
Phosphorus Deficiency	128
Potassium Deficiency	129

Introduction

Congratulations! You have made the wise decision to purchase *7 Steps To Grow Cannabis*. Now you are on your way to begin growing some big, beautiful buds. This book will guide you through the entire process of growing cannabis from seed all the way to smoke. With the information in this book, you will be able to grow your own cannabis plants indoors without some of the typical beginner headaches. You will feel confident going through the whole process. At the end of the process you will feel like a well versed cultivator.

This book focuses on growing cannabis indoors using soil or coco coir in your grow pot. I'll walk you through each step in the process and will tell you what to do and also what not to do. With the techniques in the book, it's not unheard of to get one pound of dry buds per plant. I've done it and you can too!

Growing cannabis isn't a perfect science; varying opinions exist on how to grow it. Millions of online sources exist, of which a good amount of the sources containing outdated techniques or just plain bad advice. This book is up-to-date while covering all the basics on how to grow it successfully.

This book was written so you can start at any section. I've also included a few advanced, optional techniques such as Low-Stress Training (LST), Topping and Pruning since those techniques will help you get the most yield possible.

For additional information, such as where to get seeds, a complete list of grow equipment, and grow videos, please visit my website, www.MrGrowIt.com. Also be sure to follow me on Youtube, Facebook, Instagram and Twitter @MrGrowIt for grow videos, articles, pictures, and updated information.

Happy growing,

-Mr. Grow It

Chapter 1
Equipment

EQUIPMENT

It took me quite some time to determine how I wanted to begin this book. Other cannabis grow books start off with the biology of the plant, then explain the science behind it all. Is that something that you need to know on your first run at growing cannabis? Absolutely not. Therefore, I left the boring high school biology course out of this book. This book will focus on what you need to know as someone brand new to growing cannabis plants indoors. I spent a significant amount of time thinking about how to describe the process so someone with little to no experience can easily understand and follow the steps.

Let us start from the beginning – grow equipment. Before you start growing cannabis indoors, you will need to get the tools and equipment required. Cannabis needs to be grown in certain conditions in order for the plant to be healthy and produce buds - i.e. specific temperature and humidity ranges. The equipment bought will help control the conditions of the grow environment. The grow environment is simply the surroundings or conditions that the cannabis plants are grown in. I will get more into detail on what conditions the grow environment should be in later on in this book. But for now, let's focus on equipment.

EQUIPMENT

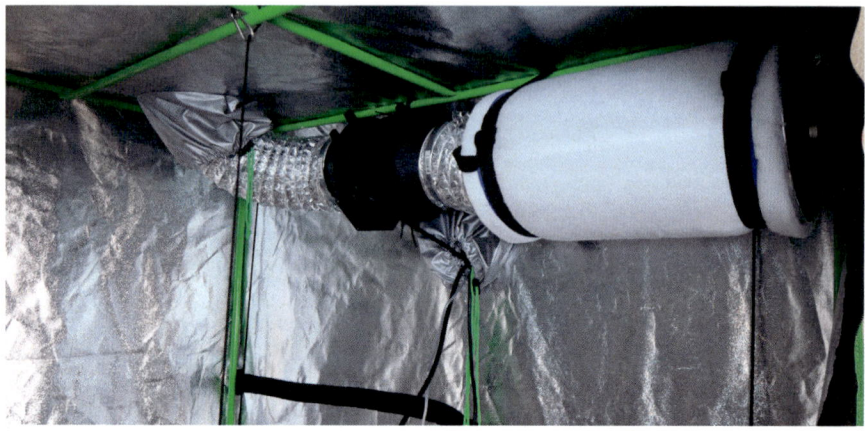

There are many different opinions on what equipment is the best and what equipment is needed vs. optional. I listed below what you will need as a minimum and then also listed some of the optional items. Some of the optional equipment you may actually need, but it all depends on the conditions of the grow environment.

- Grow Tent (optional)
- Grow Light
- Inline Fan
- Carbon Filter (optional)
- Ducting
- Oscillating Fan
- Heater (optional)
- Air Conditioner (optional)
- Humidifier (optional)
- Dehumidifier (optional)
- Grow Pot
- Soil
- Nutrients
- Temperature and Humidity Monitor
- pH Meter and TDS Tester (optional)
- Hand Pruners (optional)

EQUIPMENT

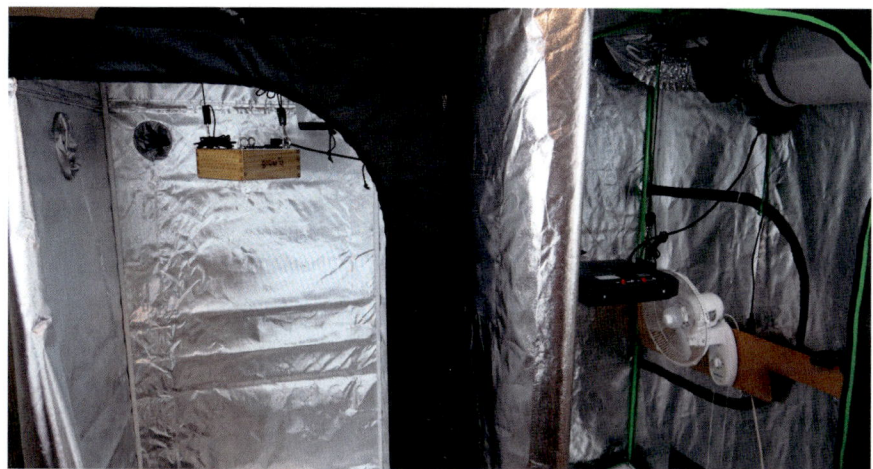

Grow TENT

I listed a grow tent as an optional item. Why? You actually do not need a grow tent. Instead, you can grow plants in a room in your house or even a small closet. However, it may be more difficult to control the conditions in your grow environment without a grow tent.

For example, plants require carbon dioxide to grow; therefore, the air in your grow environment needs to be changed every 1-3 minutes. A ventilation system will allow air to intake as well as exhaust from the grow environment. We will talk more about ventilation later on in this chapter, but know that a grow tent has exhaust vents and intake vents so a ventilation system can easily be attached to it. Without a grow tent, you may have to drill holes in your grow room wall to create an intake and exhaust to attach the ventilation system to.

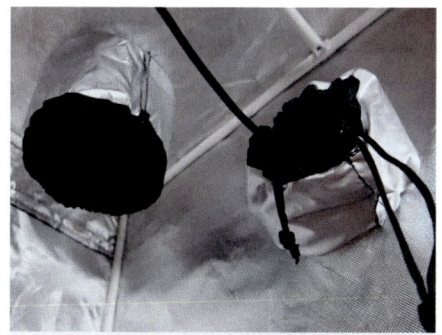

EXHAUST VENTS

INTAKE VENTS

EQUIPMENT

Since the conditions in the grow environment can be hard to control, I highly recommend growing cannabis indoors in a grow tent. But first, you will need to know how many plants you want to grow because that will determine the size of the grow tent. One medium-sized plant typically takes up about 2'x2' (60x60cm) of grow area.

4 plants in a 4'x4' (1.2x1.2m) grow tent

Let me make it easy for you with this cheat sheet...

Number of medium-sized plants	Recommended grow tent size
1-2	4' x 2' x 5' or 120 x 60 x 150cm
3-4	4' x 4' x 6.6' or 1.2 x 1.2 x 2m
5-8	8' x 4' x 6.6' or 2.4 x 1.2 x 2m

Want to grow more than 8 plants? Then you will need to either grow smaller plants or get multiple grow tents.

Be sure to know your local laws! You most likely live in an area where there is a limit to the number of cannabis plants that you can have growing at once. Most states in the United States that have legalized cannabis allow growing up to six plants. That means you can't grow more than 6 plants at any given time. In my state, I have a plant limit of 12. Under no circumstances do I recommend growing cannabis in an area where it is illegal to do so. Know your laws and abide by them!

EQUIPMENT

Now let's get back to talking about grow tents. What else do you need to know before buying a grow tent? Here are a few things that are certainly good to know:

- All grow tents have reflective Mylar on the inside which will reflect light off the walls of the grow tent and onto the plants. This helps with photosynthesis.

- The exhaust vents come in different diameters so be sure to know what diameter your grow tent vents have so you can buy a ventilation system that will fit within the grow tent.

- Grow tents with thin fabric and/or poor stitching may have light leaks. Having light leak onto your plants during their dark period can stress the plants to where they start to grow pollen sacs instead of buds! Quality is important when choosing a grow tent.

To make things easier for you, there is a section on my website dedicated to the equipment for growing cannabis. The website is always up-to-date and includes the best grow tents available right now. All items are sold through Amazon, too. You may be able to get free 2-day shipping if you have Amazon Prime. Check out my website www.MrGrowIt.com for all your grow equipment needs.

Now you know how many plants you want to grow and have a grow tent picked out. Great! Up next is lighting.

EQUIPMENT

LIGHTING

Light for plants is like food for humans – they need it to survive! Outdoor growers have the luxury of getting light free from that big bright star in the sky that we call the sun. On the other hand, indoor growers need to purchase lighting and power with electricity. This can be costly as indoor grow lights can certainly be expensive to power. Now let's talk about the types of grow lights.

There are three major types of grow lights used for indoor growing: fluorescent grow lights, high intensity discharge (HID) grow lights, and light-emitting diode (LED) grow lights. In this book, we will focus on high intensity discharge (HID) grow lights as well as light-emitting diode (LED) grow lights since these two types of grow lights will typically provide a higher yield when growing cannabis plants.

HID	vs	LED
Cheap to buy		Expensive to buy
High heat when operating		Low heat when operating
High electricity usage		Low electricity usage

EQUIPMENT

Hid
LIGHTING

High intensity discharge (HID) grow lights are arguably the most popular type of lighting for growing cannabis. This is due to the low cost to purchase (compared to LED grow lights) and the fact that one can obtain a massive yield if a HID grow light is combined with the ideal grow environment and proper feeding of nutrients. I call this the 1-2-3 knockout; execute these 3 things and knock yield out of the park!

There are three different bulbs for HID grow lights that I suggest you use when growing cannabis - Metal Halide (MH), High Pressure Sodium (HPS), and Ceramic Metal Halide (CMH). Here's what you should know about them:

Metal Halide (MH)

- Generally used during the vegetative stage of growing, but can be used throughout the entire grow and still get decent results
- Promotes vegetative growth better
- Light appears as a bluish color which replicates the spring sun

High Pressure Sodium (HPS)

- Generally used during the flowering stage of growing. But just like MH, HPS can be used throughout the entire grow
- Promotes flowering development better
- Light appears as a yellowish color which replicates the fall sun

Ceramic Metal Halide (CMH)

- Generally used throughout the entire grow
- Includes a full spectrum of light optimal for both the vegetation stage and the flowering stage

315 watt CMH grow light

EQUIPMENT

When purchasing HID grow lights, you can get a kit which will include both a MH bulb and a HPS bulb. I highly recommend you buy a grow light kit that is air cooled. HID grow lights produce a significant amount of heat and choosing an air-cooled system will make controlling the grow environment's temperature much easier.

A typical HID grow light system/ kit includes:

- 1 MH blub
- 1 HPS bulb
- Reflector (to hold the light bulb and reflect the light)
- Ballast (to power the light)
- Hangers (to hang the light)
- Timer (to automatically power the light on/off on a schedule)

Here is a list of HID grow lights (by wattage) that I recommend for different grow areas:

Air-cooled hood connected to ducting

HID grow light kit

GROW AREA	GROW LIGHT WATTAGE
4' x 2' or 3' x 3' or 120 x 60cm or 80 x 80cm	400w
4' x 4' or 1.2 x 1.2m	600w
5' x 5' or 1.5 x 1.5m	1000w
8' x 4' or 2.4 x 1.2m	2x 600w

How much will I yield using a HID grow light?

In my experience, you can expect .5 to 1 gram of dry weight per watt. Therefore, if you are using a 600w HID grow light on four plants for example, you could get 300-600 grams of bud after it properly dries. However, keep in mind that there are other factors involved that will impact yield such as environment conditions, the strain being grown, and the supply of nutrients.

EQUIPMENT

Led LIGHTING

Light-emitting diode (LED) grow lights are becoming more and more popular since they are more efficient and produce less heat than HID grow lights. However, some LED grow lights lack intensity, and therefore, many growers are adamant that HID lighting is superior to LED lighting. LED grow lights are also much more expensive than HID grow lights. I personally have made the switch from HID grow lights to LED grow lights and there were a few reasons in particular for why I made the change:

- I live in a desert region and temperature is hard to control in the summer time when it is over 100°F/38°C outside every day. Using a LED grow light has significantly lowered the temperature in my grow tent. If temperatures are too hot, plants could encounter heat stress. Do not worry. I address this and other problems in the last chapter.

- Lower electricity bill. LED grow lights provide high intensity with lower watts. At the time of writing this, there is a LED grow light which has about equal intensity to a 400w HID grow light, but the LED grow light only consumes 175w. This is a significant power savings. Because of this, I know I saved money since switching over to LED.

EQUIPMENT

> ## How much will I yield using a LED grow light?

I wish there was an easy answer to this question. This greatly depends on the intensity of the LED grow light being used. Older technology LED grow lights often produce less than .5 of a gram of dry weight per watt. Newer LED technology with high-intensity diodes can match and even beat the yield that a HID grow light can produce. But in all honesty, it is very difficult to tell you what you can expect for a yield. Variations in grow light technology, environment conditions, and nutrient uptake make it nearly impossible to estimate what yield could be. Oh, and do not forget that the strain being grown will also impact yield.

Grow lights can be expensive depending on the store selling them. Luckily, you have purchased this book and now know about my website which lists the best grow lights currently available. Check out my website www.MrGrowIt.com for an up-to-date list of the best grow lights on the market today.

EQUIPMENT

Ventilation SYSTEM

Grow tent, check. Grow light, check. What's next? Ventilation! Cannabis plants need fresh air and the air inside a grow tent or grow room should be changed every 1-3 minutes. This will allow the plants to intake carbon dioxide and execute the photosynthesis process. Thus, a fan such as an inline fan is needed to help exhaust air from the grow environment. Basically, the inline fan will pull the air from the grow environment and push it out of the grow environment. As long as one of the grow tent's intake vents are open, air will flow in when the inline fan is operating.

Inline fans come in a variety of speeds. In the United States, most inline fans have a cubic feet per minute (CFM) rating. CFM refers to how much air the fan can move each minute. You will need to make sure you are getting an inline fan that will exhaust all the air in the grow environment every 1-3 minutes. To figure out the CFM, you will need to do the math below.

First, identify the cubic area. To identify the cubic area of the grow tent or room, multiply the length by the width then by the height (in feet). For example, a 4'x4'x6.6' grow tent would have a cubic area of 106. This is the amount of air that needs to be exhausted every 1-3 minutes. Therefore, an inline fan with a CFM of 106 would change the air every minute in a 4'x4'x6.6' grow tent.

EQUIPMENT

Here is a quick cheat sheet with the math done for you:

GROW TENT	CFM
4' x 2' x 5'	40
3' x 3' x 6'	54
4' x 4' x 6.6'	106
5' x 5' x 6.6'	165
8' x 4' x 6.6'	212

Inline fans do not come with the exact CFMs as listed above so you will need to round up as necessary. I recommend getting an inline fan with a variable speed controller. A variable speed controller will allow the speed of the fan to be controlled; therefore, this gives control of the amount of air exhausting from the grow environment. You will find out later on in the Environment chapter that a variable speed controller will significantly help control the temperature and humidity in the grow environment – one of the most important aspects of growing cannabis.

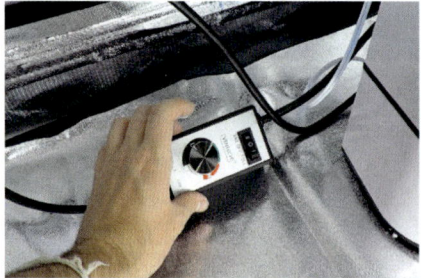

Variable speed controller   **Carbon filter w/ strapping**

Next up is the carbon filter which is an optional piece of equipment. Cannabis plants do smell (especially while in the flower stage). If you want to hide the smell, then you will certainly need a carbon filter. A carbon filter cleans the air and removes any odor in the air. Most growers will hang the carbon filter inside their grow tent by using the strapping that typically comes with a grow tent. If you do use a carbon filter, I recommend getting a higher CFM inline fan. The carbon filter will restrict air flow quite a bit so adding 100 to your CFM calculation above will help ensure you have a strong enough inline fan to change the air in the grow environment as needed.

EQUIPMENT

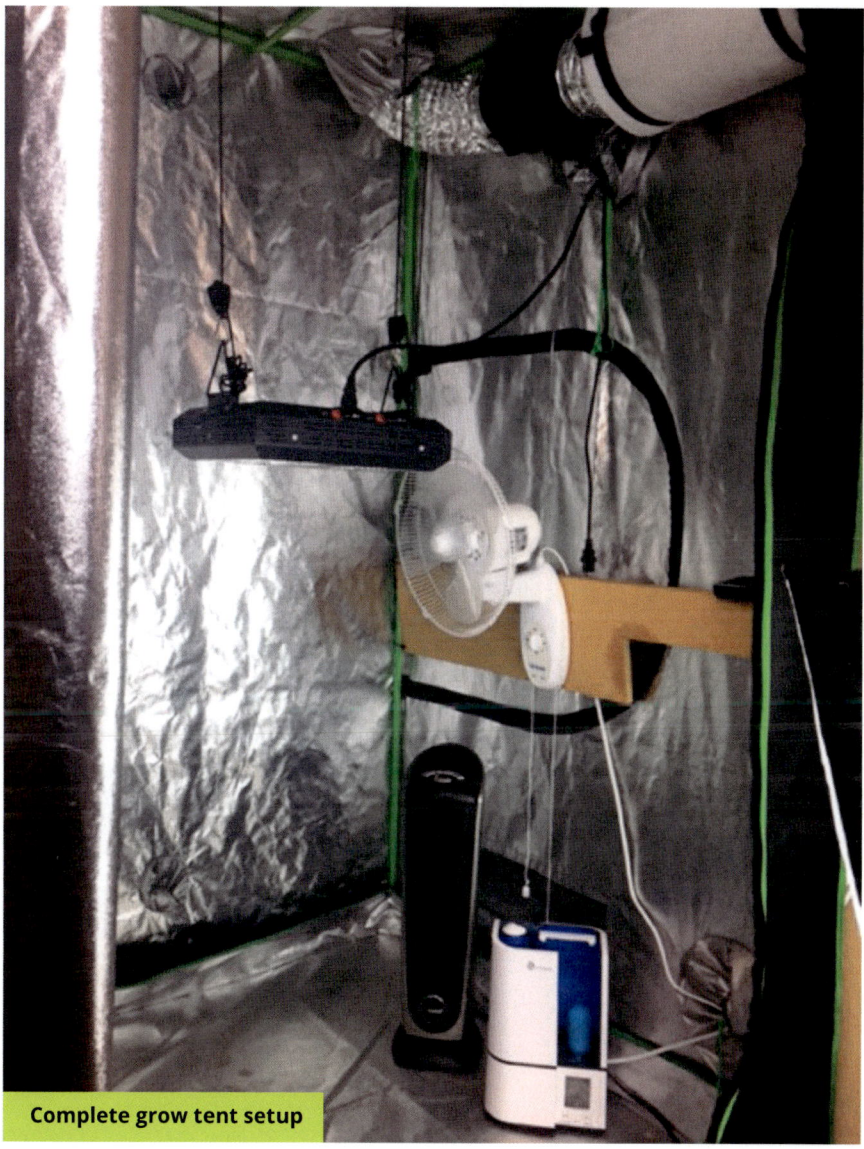

Complete grow tent setup

The last piece of the ventilation system is the ducting. The ducting connects all the pieces of the ventilation system together. Plan where to put the carbon filter and inline fan first, then measure to determine the length of ducting needed. Ducting can be cut easily to be shortened so do not worry if you cannot find the exact length you need. In the Setting Up the Equipment section of this book, I show you how to connect the ventilation system – inline fan, carbon filter, and ducting.

EQUIPMENT

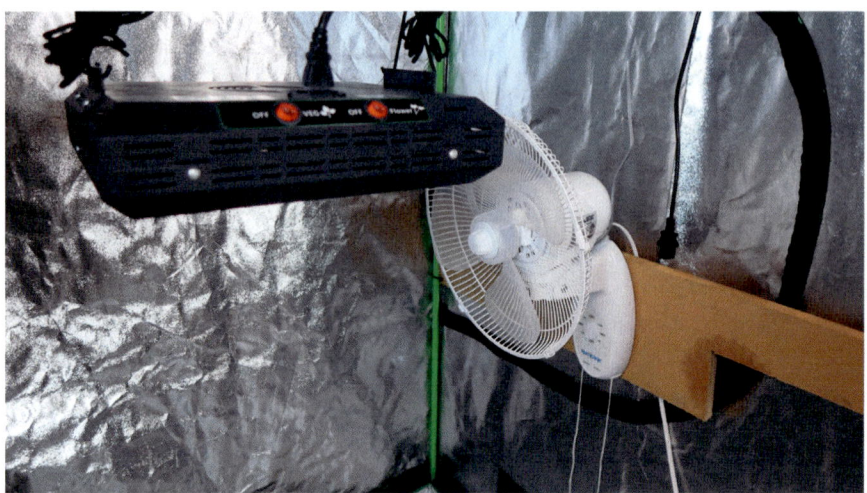

Oscillating FAN

Even with a ventilation system installed, the grow environment could get hot spots or humid pockets of air which is not good for cannabis plants. Hot spots are areas of high temperature in the grow environment. Having hot spots in the grow environment could result in the cannabis plant getting heat stress, which can certainly hinder the growth of the plant. Even more harmful, humid pockets, or areas of high humidity in the grow environment, can result in powdery mildew forming on the plant. Powdery mildew can destroy the plant and make you sick if you smoke buds with mildew on them. Therefore, proper air circulation in the grow environment is a must. You will want at least one fan that oscillates inside of the grow space. Having an oscillating fan in the grow environment will also help strengthen the plant's branches since the air circulation will be forcing the plants to sway. This replicates the plant's natural outdoor environment. Strong branches will be important for the plant especially in the flower stage when buds start to form. Depending on the cannabis strain being grown, the plant could grow buds so big and heavy that the branches cannot support them and instead flop over to the ground. Strong branches will help prevent that from happening.

EQUIPMENT

Grow POT

A grow pot or plant pot is a container that is used for growing plants. They come in many different sizes and choosing the right ones can be tricky if you are new to growing cannabis. In order to determine the grow pot size to use, I recommend you answer the following

QUESTIONS:

1. Am I growing an autoflower plant or a photoperiod plant?

2. How tall do I expect my plant to grow?

Autoflower plant? Photoperiod plant? What are those? We get into exactly what autoflower and photoperiod plants are in the next chapter, when we talk about seeds. Therefore, if you do not know the difference between the two types of plants, skip to that section now, read it, and then come back here to finishing learning about what grow pot sizes to use.

Now that you know the difference between autoflower plants and photoperiod plants, let's talk about what grow pots I recommend to grow cannabis plants in.

EQUIPMENT

If you have decided to grow an autoflower plant, your job of picking out a grow pot size just got a little bit easier. Autoflower plants are often recommended for beginners because they are easier to grow in some ways. One of the reasons why they are easier to grow is because it is recommended to plant autoflower seeds into a grow pot and then keep it in that same grow pot for the entire life of the plant – so no transplanting. Autoflower cannabis plants will automatically start to flower when the plant is around 30 days old. If the plant is transplanted, there is risk that the plant could encounter transplant shock which will slow the growth of the plant. The slowed growth could result in a lower yield. Due to this, I recommend growing autoflower plants in either a 3, 4, or 5-gallon grow pot and keep it in that grow pot for its entire life.

If you are growing a photoperiod plant, I recommend you start growing it in a small container such as a 16 oz. plastic cup. When the plant grows to approximately 6" tall, transplant the plant to a 1 gallon grow pot. Wait for more growth and then transplant again to the final grow pot which I recommend to be a 3, 4, or 5-gallon grow pot. When I say final grow pot, I mean the grow pot that it will be in for the remainder of its life. With photoperiod plants, you control how long the plant is in the vegetation stage. If the plant were to encounter transplant shock after being transplanted, the plant can have time to recover before being forced into the flowering stage. Are you lost yet? Don't worry. We talk more in detail about the transplanting process in the Vegetation chapter and more about forcing the plant into the flowering stage in the Flower chapter.

A bigger grow pot will hold more soil. Soil can be expensive so going with a smaller grow pot may save you money. However, since the smaller grow pots do not hold as much soil, that means they do not hold as much water either. I have grown cannabis plants in 3 and 5-gallon grow pots side-by-side and quickly came to the realization that when my plants were in the flowering stage, I needed to water the plant in the 3-gallon grow pot daily. The plant in the 5-gallon grow pot could be watered every other day – and sometimes even every three days. So, if you are going with a 3-gallon grow pot, expect to water more frequently.

Another factor to consider is the height of the plant. Let me debunk one of the myths about cannabis plant height. I heard many people say that if a plant is grown in a 1-gallon grow pot, then you can expect the plant to grow to be approximately 1-foot tall. Growing a plant in a 3-gallon grow pot would result in a 3-foot tall plant, and a plant in a 5-gallon grow pot would result in a 5-foot tall plant. This is false. The type of cannabis strain being grown will greatly influence its height – not the size of the grow pot being used. Additionally, how long the plant is kept in the vegetation stage will also be a factor in how tall the plant can grow. However, I do like using this "gallon = height" theory as a target. Want to grow a 1-foot tall plant? You can do that successfully in a 1-gallon container. Want to grow a 3-foot tall plant? I recommend a 3-gallon container for that. So on and so forth. Just know that the container size will not always equal the height of the plant.

EQUIPMENT

PLASTIC GROW POTS	vs	FABRIC GROW POTS
Lower cost		Higher cost
Higher heat in root zone		Releases heat
Roots circle in grow pot		Prevents circling roots
More susceptible to drought		Aerates the root zone

There are a few different types of grow pots that you can use to grow a plant in. Let's quickly talk about the two most common – plastic grow pots and fabric grow pots.

Plastic grow pots are cheaper than fabric grow pots and plants will grow just fine if you use them. An important factor to consider is that roots like cool and moist conditions and plastic pots can get fairly warm (especially under grow lights). When roots grow to the edge of a plastic pot, there is a small layer of water and nutrients between the growing medium and the walls of the grow pot. As roots' sole purpose is to hunt out food and water, the plant is tricked into thinking there is still space for it to grow even while it is wrapping around the edges inside the plastic grow pot. The roots that are circling around the inside of the edge are more susceptible to excess heat, drought, and disease – all 3 can hinder the growth of the plant.

Fabric grow pots were later developed and will give better results. These grow pots have several additional benefits such as: releases heat, prevents circling roots, air-prunes the plant's root structure, and aerates the root zone. On the downside, fabric grow pots come in at a slightly higher cost and may need to be replaced after a few grows. The choice is yours.

Growing
MEDIUM & NUTRIENTS

There are several different types of growing mediums that you can utilize to successfully grow cannabis. A growing medium can be defined as a substance through which roots grow and extract water and nutrients. A few examples of growing mediums are soil, coco coir, Rockwool, and perlite. There are several others, but you do not need to know them all since we are focusing on the two most common – soil and coco coir. Soil and coco coir are the two easiest growing mediums to use for growing cannabis. Let's talk a little more about both of those mediums – starting with soil.

When choosing a soil, know that all soils have what is called a Nitrogen-Phosphorus-Potassium (NPK) ratio. For growing cannabis, you will want to get a soil that has an NPK ratio of around 5:1:1 or 8:4:4. The first number represents nitrogen, the second number represents phosphorus and the third number represents potassium. In other words, any soil composed of more nitrogen than the other two nutrients will be adequate. Another aspect to investigate when buying soil is the pH of the soil. A soil with a pH between 6.0-7.0 is good for growing cannabis. I recommend FoxFarm Ocean Forest soil since the pH is adjusted (6.3 to 6.8) which allows for optimum nutrient uptake. This is one of the reasons why FoxFarm Ocean Forest is good for beginners. Another reason that it is good for beginners is because this brand of soil already has nutrients mixed in so you will not need to feed the plant bottled nutrients for the first 20-40 days of the plant's life.

EQUIPMENT

When choosing coco coir, there are two main options – brick and pre-mixed. A brick of coco coir is simply that – a brick. Bricks of coco coir require prep prior to growing cannabis in them. They first need to be soaked in water so the brick expands and breaks apart. Then the brick should be buffered with calcium and magnesium prior to using. This buffering process is very time consuming and I do not recommended beginners to take this route. The easier route is to go with a pre-mixed bag of coco coir. Nearly all pre-mixed bags of coco coir are already buffered and are ready to use. Pre-mixed bags do cost more than bricks, although, the time you save not having to buffer is well worth the few extra bucks.

A brick of coco coir

Coco coir ready for use

Soaking a brick of coco coir

EQUIPMENT

In addition to the growing medium, you will need nutrients to feed the plant. No matter which growing medium you choose, I recommend Blue Planet Nutrients trio line of nutrients – Grow, Micro, and Bloom. This pack of 3 bottles provide almost everything needed for the entire grow. The only other thing you will most likely need is a calcium and magnesium additive (which is called CalMag). If you choose to grow in coco coir, with a LED grow light, or are using reverse osmosis (RO) water, you will definitely need CalMag. Cannabis plants tend to intake more calcium and magnesium when growing in coco coir and/or under a LED grow light. Also, if using RO water, the filter will catch the calcium and magnesium so it will not be in the water. The amount of nutrients you feed the cannabis plant will vary throughout the plant's life. I have provided more details on feeding the plant in the Feeding Nutrients section of this book.

There are several other options for growing mediums and nutrients out there. There are also additives that you can feed the plant such as: silica, PK boosters, and microbial inoculants. Those additives are not needed. Those additives do increase the health of the plant in various ways, but I do not recommend using them if you are a beginner since it adds complexity to the feeding process. Remember, my recommendations consist of products that I have used and know work well. Feel free to conduct your own research and choose a different growing medium and/or nutrients as you wish.

Humidifier, Dehumidifier, HEATER, AIR CONDITIONER

Humidifier, dehumidifier, heater, and air conditioner are grow equipment that I've listed as optional, however, they may actually be needed. It really all depends on the grow environment conditions. For example, I currently live in southern Nevada which is a desert region. It is always very dry (low humidity) here and when I first started growing cannabis in this area, I ran into humidity issues – my humidity was too low! Since my grow environment was so dry, I needed to buy a humidifier and have it running almost 24/7. On the other hand, if you live in a humid environment such as the Northwest region of the United States, you will probably need a dehumidifier instead in order to reduce the humidity.

If you need a humidifier or dehumidifier, make sure there is a feature on the unit where the humidity level can be set. That way, the equipment will automatically turn on when the humidity level is out of range. A grow environment with low humidity can stunt a plant's growth. A grow environment with high humidity can lead to powdery mildew, bud rot, and mold. The ideal humidity level will change throughout the life of the plant. We get into more detail on what humidity range the grow environment should be in, for each stage of the plant's life, in the Environment chapter.

EQUIPMENT

Heater

Humidifier

Now let's talk a little bit about the temperature in the grow environment and the equipment you can use to help control it. You will learn in the Environment chapter that the ideal temperature range for growing cannabis is between 70-80°F/21-27°C if using HID lighting and 75-85°F/24-30°C if using LED lighting. Typically, in the winter time or even at night time (when the grow lights are off), many grow environments fall below 70°F/21°C. It is ok if the temperature falls down to as low as 60°F/16°C range during the last few weeks of the grow since it replicates late fall outdoor growing. However, if the grow environment frequently drops into the 60°F/16°C range, then the plant could encounter problems. In that case, the best fix is to get a portable heater. I recommend getting a portable heater with a temperature setting so that the heater will automatically turn on if the grow environment temperature falls below the temperature set on the heater. Then, of course, when the grow environment increases to the temperature set on the heater, the heater will automatically turn off. Automation in the grow room such as this will certainly make the process of growing cannabis much easier.

EQUIPMENT

Curling leaves is a sign of heat stress

Foxtailing due to heat stress

You may be wondering: What if the temperature in the grow environment is above the ideal temperature range? Well, if you live in a hot environment and cannot keep the grow environment under 80°F/27°C (when using HID lighting) or 85°F/30°C (when using LED lighting), then you will need to add an air conditioner to the grow environment in order to pump cool air into it. If the environment's temperature is too hot, the plant will encounter heat stress. This will certainly negatively impact the plant's overall yield.

I said it a few times so far in this book and I will say it again (this will be the last time – I promise!). There is an up-to-date list of the best grow equipment (including a humidifier, dehumidifier, heater, and air conditioner) on my website www.MrGrowIt.com

EQUIPMENT

Setting Up
THE EQUIPMENT

You have all the equipment you need. Now you need to set it up. After you complete this, most of the decision making will be done, and then it is just a matter of following the process of growing.

Ready? Let's go!

Start with the grow tent. First, remember that the air in the grow tent will need to be changed every 1-3 minutes. The tent intakes air, and then will exhaust out of the grow tent. On most grow tents, there are one or more rectangle openings near the bottom of the tent. Those are the intake vents. Make sure when you assemble the grow tent that you position the tent so that at least one intake vent is not blocked by anything. For example, do not place the grow tent next to a wall. This would result in the intake vent being blocked.

The circular vents on the upper part of the grow tent are for the exhaust. Similar to the intake, you will need to make sure there is nothing blocking at least one of the exhaust vents so you can properly install the ventilation system to it. I recommend that the exhaust vent that you use be on the opposite side of the open intake vent. Therefore, the ventilation system will be diagonal to the intake vent. This will help with air circulation across the grow tent.

EQUIPMENT

Exhaust vents

Intake vent

Next, use the strapping included with the grow tent to hang the carbon filter on one of the top bars of the grow tent. After that, secure the inline fan after the carbon filter, on the same top bar of the tent. Then, run the ducting from the carbon filter to the inline fan and then more ducting from the inline fan through the exhaust vent. From there, I recommended the ducting to go into another room, into an attic, or out of a window. If you simply exhaust the hot air from the grow environment into the room the grow tent is in, then that hot air could recirculate back into the grow tent. This will make controlling the temperature in the grow tent much more difficult.

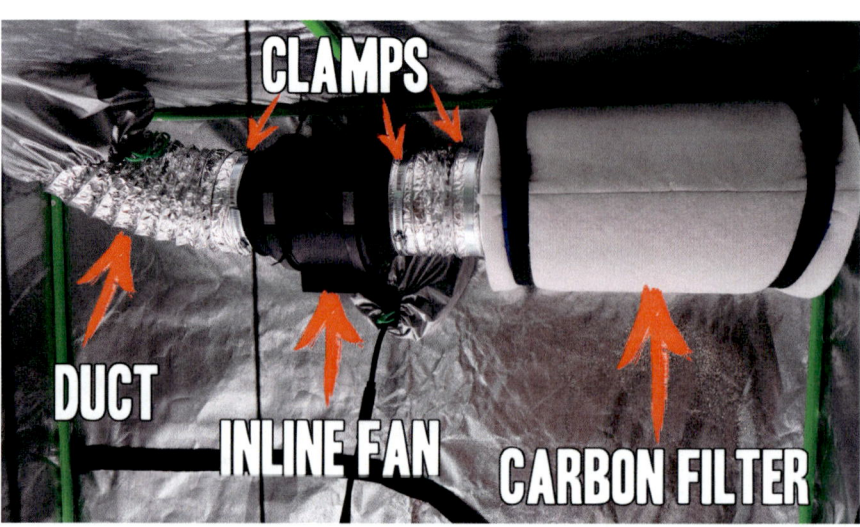

EQUIPMENT

Air-cooled reflector connected to ventilation system

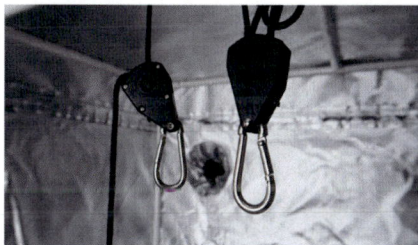
Light ratchets

Oscillating fan mounted in grow tent

If you are using an air-cooled reflector for HID lighting, connect the ventilation system to the grow light as pictured to the right. This will help remove the heat from the grow environment that is produced by the HID grow light.

The grow light should be hung in the middle of the grow tent, and I recommend using light ratchets that are adjustable. Using adjustable light ratchets will make it much easier to move the light up as the plants grow. If using HID lighting, the light ballast can be mounted either inside or outside of the grow tent. Ballasts give off heat so if you mount it outside of the tent, then there will be one less source of heat inside of the tent.

Place or mount the oscillating fan inside the environment. Air should blow onto the plant but there should not be a constant wind. Too much consistent wind on the plant could result in the plant getting wind burn. As the fan oscillates, it should blow air onto different parts of the plant at different times.

EQUIPMENT

Heater and humidifier inside a grow tent

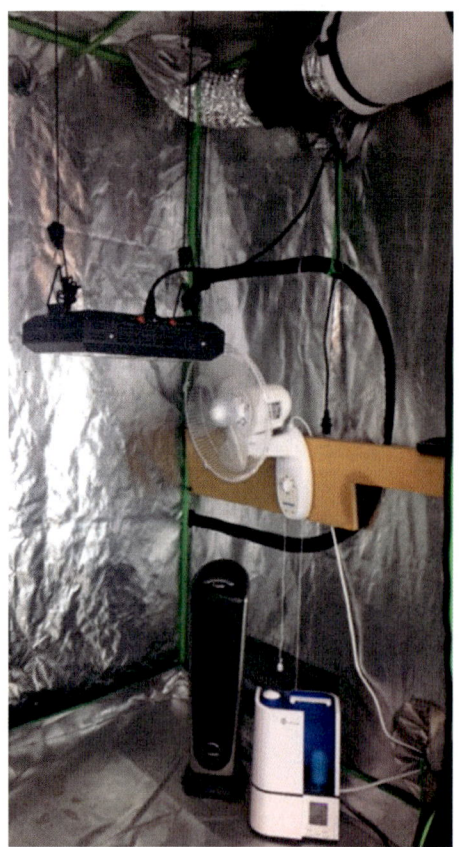

Complete grow tent setup

You can place the heater and humidifier inside or outside the grow environment. If placed inside, you may run into space constraints as the plant grows so it is probably best to put those pieces of equipment outside of the grow tent near an intake vent to give the plant more room. If you are using a dehumidifier or an air conditioner, I recommend placing them outside of the grow tent by one of the intake vents.

At this point, you should now have all of the grow equipment set up and be ready to start growing cannabis. But before you can start growing, you will need seeds. Step 1 complete; now onto step 2.

Chapter 2
Seeds

GETTING SEEDS

I n order to start the process of growing cannabis, you will need either a cannabis seed or a clone of a cannabis plant. Since the cloning process is a more advanced technique, it is not covered in this book. Instead, we focus on growing cannabis from seeds. In this chapter, we will cover getting seeds, bag seeds, the types of seeds, germinating seeds, and planting seeds.

When it comes to buying cannabis seeds, laws vary by country. To make things even more complex, some countries have individual states that have their own laws on cannabis. This can make the process of buying cannabis seeds very confusing for consumers. Typically, in areas where cannabis is legal for either medical or recreational purposes, cannabis seeds can be purchased at local dispensaries. Some consumers resort to online seed banks to have cannabis seeds shipped directly to their home. This may worry some growers, but know that most seed banks are reliable and safe. Do not buy cannabis seeds if it is not legal for you to do so! You are responsible for complying with the laws in your state/country. I am not a lawyer; therefore, I'm not able to provide you any legal advice. I do not condone breaking the law.

Now that I've discussed what to legally consider before buying seeds, let's talk about seed banks. Seed banks take buyer's discretion extremely seriously. They do not just toss cannabis seeds into a bag, pack them in a brown box, and then ship the box to you. They typically offer what is called stealth shipping. Stealth shipping is where they carefully hide seeds within another item. For example, someone I know, we will call him John, once ordered seeds from an overseas seed bank. A package came to his house two weeks later. He opened the package and pulled out a white t-shirt that read "London" in large colorful letters across the top of the t-shirt. After he pulled out the t-shirt, he looked back in the package and nothing was in there. John

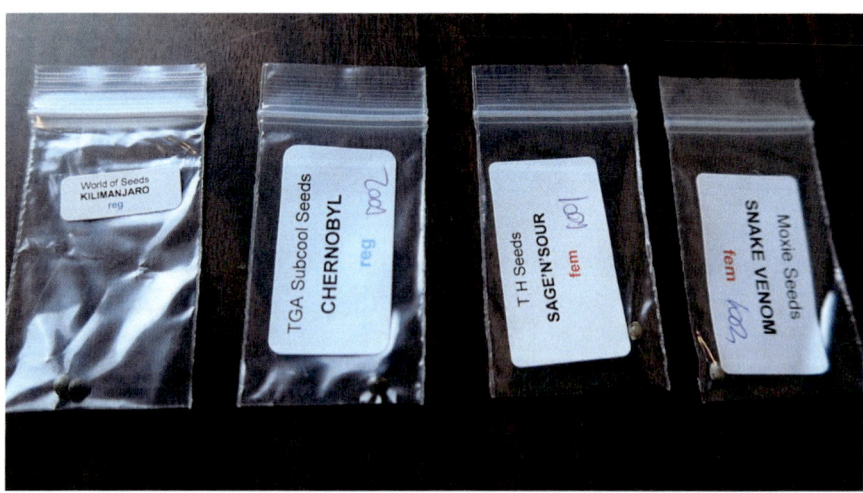

thought to himself, "What the heck! I got ripped off!" Immediately after that, he unfolded the t-shirt hoping that seeds would fall out…nothing fell out. John frantically turned the t-shirt inside out and voila! The seeds were in a tiny bag taped to the inside of the t-shirt by the shoulder. Seed banks are frequently switching up their stealth methods, but it is comforting knowing that the seeds are well hidden resulting in less chances of being confiscated by Customs and Border Protection.

> ## What if Customs and Border Protection were to find seeds? What happens?

Out of the ten years I have been growing, I have only heard of this happening to one person. That person chose not to get the stealth shipping option that the seed bank offered for an additional $5. Customs and Border Protection sidelined his package. They opened the package, found the seeds, and replaced them with an official letter signed by Customs and Border Protection. The letter stated that the seeds were confiscated. Out of everyone I know in the cannabis community, this was the only instance (shared with me) detailing that Customs and Border Protection confiscated seeds. I have never heard about someone's house being raided due to seeds being found at customs. Frankly, I assume that they have bigger fish to fry and won't go busting down your door over a 10-pack of seeds.

Be patient! I mentioned that it took John two weeks to receive his package of seeds from the seed bank, but that is considered fast. Depending on where you live and the location of the seed bank, it could take up to a month or longer to receive them. November and December seem to take the longest due to the holidays in those months. If you do not receive your seeds after a month, contact the seed bank. They will either have you wait a few more weeks or typically send you out more seeds – free of charge. Be careful! Some seed websites are actually scams! For an updated list of reputable seed banks, visit my website www.MrGrowIt.com

Bag SEEDS

Some of you may be wondering if you can use bag seeds. For those of you who do not know what I mean by bag seeds, I am talking about the seeds that you randomly find in your bag of weed. The short answer is yes, but it is not recommended. I do not recommend it because if you are finding seeds within your buds, that means that particular plant could be a hermaphrodite aka a hermie. A hermaphrodite cannabis plant has both male and female characteristics. The plant will grow both buds as well as pollen sacs. Hermaphrodite cannabis plants typically have a lower potency and will result in a lower yield since the plant is focusing a lot of its energy on producing pollen sacs instead of buds. Additionally, the final dry buds will have seeds in them which will need to be removed prior to smoking. Seeds should not be smoked since there are no trichomes with THC attached to them and they won't get you high. If you plant bag seeds, the chance of those seeds growing and becoming a hermie is extremely high since they are the same genetics as the hermie plant they came from. You will learn more about hermaphrodite plants in the Sexing section of this book.

SEEDS

Types of SEEDS

Autoflower vs Photoperiod

Before you buy seeds, you will want to have some knowledge on the different types of seeds. To break it down for you, there are two major types of cannabis plants – autoflower and photoperiod. Autoflower plants stay on the same light cycle for the entire grow and will automatically go into the flower stage at or around day 30. Photoperiod plants will not go into the flower stage until the light cycle is changed to 12-12 (12 hours lights on, and 12 hours lights off).

Regular vs Feminized

Both Autoflower and Photoperiod seeds are listed as either Regular or Feminized. Regular seeds are seeds that after they are planted and start to grow, will become either male or female. As for feminized seeds, they always end up being a female plant because they are bred a certain way by the seed breeder. You will learn more about male and female plants in the Sexing section of this book. Both autoflower seeds and feminized seeds are typically more expensive than regular photoperiod seeds.

Indoor vs Outdoor

Some seed banks will also separate their seeds into Indoor and Outdoor categories. The difference between the two is straightforward – indoor seeds grow better indoors and outdoor seeds grow better outdoors. Yes, you can grow outdoor seeds indoors and vice versa; however, you may not get the same results that the seed bank lists in their listing description for that particular seed. i.e. plant might be shorter, have a lower THC percentage, etc.

Indica vs Sativa

The last thing to know when buying seeds is Indica vs. Sativa. I won't go into every detail about the difference between the two, but I will talk about a few main characteristics. First, the appearance of the plants. Sativa plants are tall, loosely branched and have long, narrow leaves. They are usually grown outdoors and can reach heights of up to 20 feet. Indica plants are short, densely branched and have wider leaves. The effects felt after smoking them is different as well. Sativa plants produce more of an uplifting and energetic high. It can also be cerebral, spacey, or hallucinogenic. Due to these effects, Sativa is best suited for day use. Indica plants produce a relaxing and calming high. Some call an Indica high a body buzz or "couch lock" because it's more of a narcotic high. Accordingly, Indica is best suited for night use.

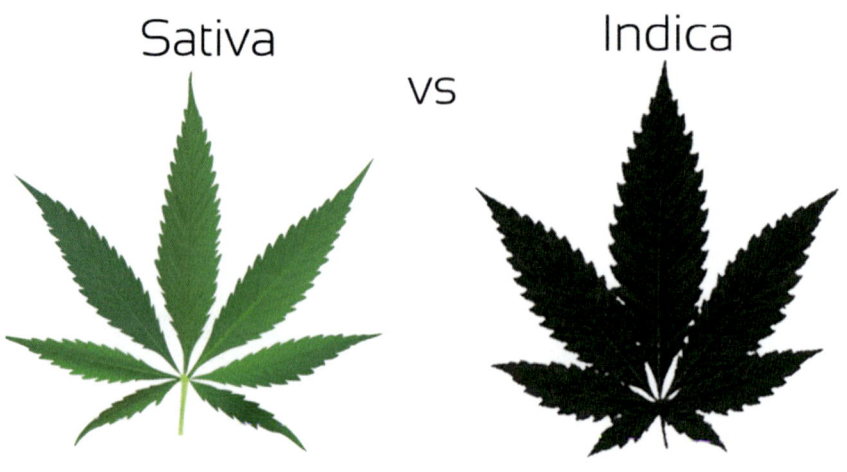

Germinating SEEDS

Once you have a cannabis seed, you can start the germination process. Germination is the process that involves causing a seed to sprout. A sprout is a new growth of a plant. Under the ideal conditions, the seed will crack open and a root will appear. This root is often called a taproot. There are many ways to germinate cannabis seeds. In this book I will teach you one of the easiest methods – the paper towel method.

Is the paper towel method mandatory? No, it's not. You can skip this process and plant the seed directly into the growing medium. However, the seed may not sprout for various reasons. Due to this, most growers prefer germinating their seeds prior to planting them in the growing medium. This allows you to confirm that the seed sprouted from its shell instead of planting it in the soil and waiting day after day only to realize the seed was bad. Germinating the seed prior to planting could save you time. If you are going to plant your seed prior to germinating, skip this section and move onto the Planting Seeds section.

For the paper towel method, gather the following items for each seed:

- 1 small cup (a shot glass is perfect)
- 1 paper towel
- 1 small plate
- 1 plastic bag (optional)
- Water (any type - tap, distilled, reverse osmosis)

First, put water in the small cup. If you are using a shot glass you can fill it about ¾ full. Not much water is needed here. You can use any type of water for this process – tap, distilled, reverse osmosis, etc. The water does not need to be a specific pH or have a certain PPM. Not sure what pH and PPM are? Don't worry. There are sections on pH and PPM in this book. You will learn about them a little later on.

Next, drop the seed into the cup of water. The water should be room temperature. The seed may float in the water. If it sinks, then you may have a bad seed – but do not panic just yet. That seed might still be good. Use your finger to push down the seed into the water in attempt for it to sink. Some seeds will sink right away with a little push but most seeds should pop right back up and float. Put the cup in a dark place and let the seed float on the water for 18-24 hours.

Drop seeds into a cup of water

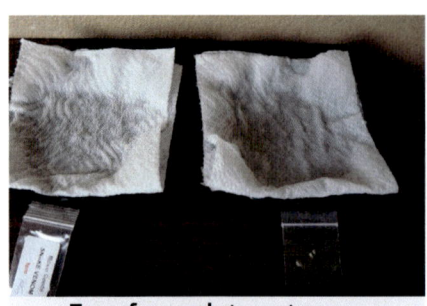
Transfer seeds to wet paper towel then cover

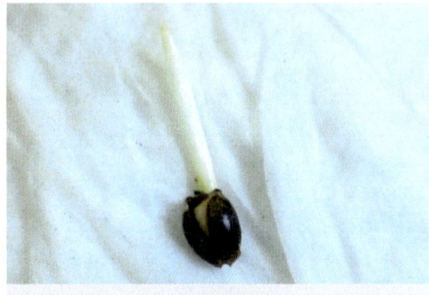
Tap root emerging from seed

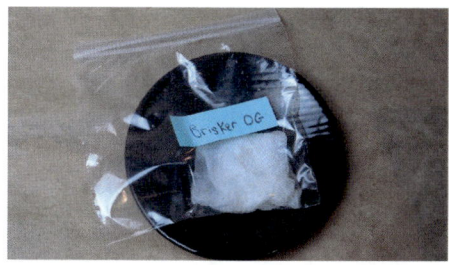

After the seed has sat in the water for 18-24 hours, it's time to transfer the seed to a paper towel. Place a paper towel onto a small plate. Pour the cup of water with the seed onto the paper towel. If you are germinating several seeds, spread the seeds out on the paper towel so they aren't close to each other and fold over the paper towel to cover the seeds. The paper towel will absorb the water. You can then either leave the wet paper towel on the plate or put it in a plastic bag. If you put it in a plastic bag, do not seal the bag. Placing the paper towel in a plastic bag is optional but it does help retain moisture. You must keep the paper towel moist for the remainder of the process. Put it in a dark place that is room temperature and let it sit for approximately 24 hours.

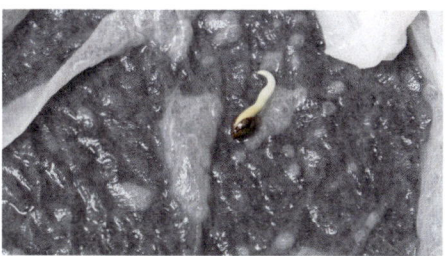

After 24 hours, open the paper towel. If the seed has cracked open and the tap root is at least ¼ inch long, you are ready to move onto the next process which is planting the seed. If the tap root isn't ¼ inch long, fold up the paper towel and put it back into the plastic bag. Remember to keep the paper towel moist at all times. Check on the seed every 24 hours until the tap root is at least ¼ inch long. Once your seed has germinated, you are ready to move onto the next process which is planting the seed.

What happens if my seed doesn't germinate?

Not all seeds will germinate. If your seed hasn't cracked open after being in the paper towel for 72 hours then it's probably a bad seed.

Planting
SEEDS

If you got to this point, that means you have either successfully completed the paper towel method or you have skipped that process (and are going to take the risk of planting the seed directly in the medium without first germinating). In this section we will go over what grow pot size to use, how to plant a seed, and the conditions you should put your seedling in.

First, let's talk about grow pot size. Are you planting an autoflower seed or a photoperiod seed? If you are planting an autoflower seed, I highly recommend you plant the seed directly into a large container such as a 3-gallon, 4-gallon, or 5-gallon grow pot. Why? To avoid the transplanting process. The transplanting process can cause a stunt in growth. Any stunt in growth for autoflower plants will negatively impact yield since you can't control how long autoflowers live like you can with photoperiod plants.

If you have a photoperiod seed, I recommend planting it in a small plastic cup to begin. Slice the bottom corners of the plastic cup in 8-10 places so that water can drain through the cup. Once the plant grows big enough, you will transplant into a larger container. I explain the transplanting process in detail in the Transplanting section of this book.

Cut slices in the bottom of the plastic cup for drainage

Fill the cup with soil but leave an inch of space

Create a small hole about 1/8 to 1/4 inch deep

SEEDS

Place seed into the hole tap root down

After you've determined what grow pot size to use, fill the grow pot with medium but not all the way to the top. If planting in a small plastic cup, leave an inch between the medium and top of the cup. If planting in a larger grow pot, leave about 2 inches between the medium and top of the grow pot. You want this extra space in order to avoid overflow when watering.

Stick your finger in the middle of the medium to create a small hole about 1/8 to 1/4 inch deep. Any deeper than that and the seed might not sprout. Use tweezers or gloves to pick up the seed. Try not to touch the root at all; the oils on your fingers could harm the root! Place into the hole with the tap root pointing down. Then, lightly cover the seed with the medium – do not pack the medium down. Use a spray bottle to spray the top of the medium so it's moist.

After covering the seed, spray the top of the medium with water

Placing a plastic bag over the cup will help keep humidity up

SEEDS

Remove plastic bag once the seed sprouts from the medium

Place the plastic cup or grow pot in your grow environment and turn on your grow light. If you are using MH/HPS lighting, you should have the MH bulb in and turn the knob on the ballast down to the lowest setting which is typically in the range of 100w-250w. The grow light should be a distance of 24"-36" away from the top of the container. If you are using a LED grow light, the recommended light distance from the top of the container is typically 24"-36". However, every LED grow light is different. The intensity of LED grow lights vary greatly and the manufacturer may recommend a different distance.

Always follow the manufacturer's recommended light distance. A grow light too close to your seedling could burn it, which would kill it. I've made that mistake before! Place a temperature and humidity monitor next to the grow pot so it is at soil level. The soil level temperature should be between 72-82°F/22-28°C and the humidity should be in the range of 65- 85%. If you are having trouble getting the grow environment up to 65-85% humidity, place a plastic bag or plastic wrap over the cup or grow pot for the first 24-48 hours. This will help get the humidity up to the ideal range.

Check on the seedling every 3-4 hours and spray the top of the medium to keep it moist. Do not let the medium dry out. It can take anywhere from a couple of hours to a couple of days before you see the young seedling pop out from the medium. If the seedling has not sprouted from the medium within ten days after being planted, unfortunately, it probably will not survive.

CHEAT SHEET - FIRST TWO WEEKS AFTER SPROUT	
Temperature (at soil level)	72-82°F/22-28°C
Humidity	65-85%
Light cycle	18-6 (18 hours on, 6 hours off)
Light distance (from top of pot/plant)	24"-36" for HID and ask manufacturer for LED

Seedlings 10 days after sprouting from the medium

TEMPERATURE

The conditions of your grow environment are imperative to growing cannabis successfully. Therefore, I consider this chapter as one of the most important – even though it is the shortest chapter in this book. Do not take this chapter lightly. Maintaining ideal temperature and humidity can be extremely difficult. If you cannot keep these key pieces where they need to be, you could destroy your entire crop. In this chapter, we will focus on temperature, humidity, air circulation, and properly balancing those conditions in your grow environment.

Let's start with temperature. The temperature in the grow environment will need to be in a specific range throughout the entire grow. If you are growing with a HID grow light, that range is 70-80°F/21-27°C. If you are growing with an LED grow light, that range is 75-85°F/24-30°C. One of your main goals when growing cannabis is to keep the temperature in that ideal range. Additionally, you do not want the temperature to swing more than 15°F/7°C. Large swings in temperature stresses cannabis plants which can sometimes cause plants to become hermaphrodite.

What if the temperature goes above the ideal range?

If the temperature goes above the ideal range, the plant could experience heat stress. The leaves will start to curl upwards like a taco and the growth of the plant will slow down. If the plant is in the flower stage and has buds, the top of the buds closest to the grow light may turn white. This is called light bleaching. Additionally, the plant could start to foxtail. Foxtailing is when buds start to form on top of each other to look like little towers. We will go over more details on heat-related problems and how to fix them in the Problems chapter of this book.

What if the temperature drops below the ideal range?

It is normal for the temperature to drop when the lights are off in your grow environment. Think about plants growing outdoors. Naturally, the temperature drops when the sun goes down. Thus, it is recommended that the temperature drops when growing indoors as well. Keep in mind, the plant can encounter stress if the temperature drops too low. If the temperature drops below the ideal range, you may see the stems start to turn purple. This is an indication that the plant is stressed; consequently, the plant's growth will slow down. The plant is focusing its energy on strengthening its stems rather than growing tall and producing buds.

HUMIDITY

The next important condition in your grow environment is relative humidity (RH). To put it simply, relative humidity is the amount of water vapor in the air and it's stated as a percentage. The ideal RH percent for a cannabis plant changes throughout the life of the plant. When the plant has just sprouted above ground, its root structure is very small. A high humidity environment during this stage will help the plant to develop a larger root structure. As the plant grows and has an established root structure, the humidity in your grow environment doesn't need to be as high.

Advanced growers will actually keep the humidity in their grow environment high throughout their entire grow. This is a more advanced and risky technique that's called Vapor Pressure Deficit (VPD). I'll try to make this simple for you. VPD is the difference between pressures of water vapor held in the air being measured at the same given temperature. This is confusing to most growers and VPD isn't something that a beginner will follow. However, I did want to mention it in this book for your awareness. Running high humidity in your grow environment could lead to things such as powdery mildew, bud rot, and mold if you don't have proper air circulation. That's the main reason why it's risky and more for advanced growers. VPD is optimal, but not required.

ENVIRONMENT

The reality is that cannabis can be grown in a wide-range of humidity levels. Here is a cheat sheet which shows the ideal humidity ranges that I recommend for beginner cannabis growers:

STAGE	IDEAL HUMIDITY RANGE
Weeks 1 & 2 in seedling/vegetation stage	65-85%
Weeks 3+ in vegetation stage	45-65%
Weeks 1-3 in flower stage	40-55%
Weeks 4+ in flower stage	30-50%
Two weeks before harvest	As low as possible

As you can see by looking at the cheat sheet, the ideal humidity range for cannabis is high when the plant is young and lowers as the plant gets older. Two weeks before harvest, I recommended lowering the humidity in your grow environment. As stated in the chart, make the grow environment as dry as possible in the last two weeks. This helps stress the plant towards the end of its life and in result, the plant will focus its energy on ripening its buds.

What if the humidity goes outside of the ideal range?

If the humidity in the grow environment goes outside of the ideal range for a temporary period of time then the plant will most likely be ok. However, if the humidity is consistently out of the ideal range, then you are at risk of things such as slowed growth, powdery mildew, bud rot, and mold. Moreover, the plant may become so stressed that it becomes a hermaphrodite. Most of these problems will completely destroy the plant. That is why it is crucial to keep your grow environment in the ideal humidity range.

ENVIRONMENT

Air CIRCULATION

Another key component you will need to control in your grow environment is air circulation. Without air circulation in your grow environment, hot spots and humid spots could form. You just learned in the previous two sections problems that can occur from too high or too low temperature and humidity in a grow environment. Simply adding an oscillating fan into your grow environment can help prevent some of those problems. For example, if the humidity in your grow environment exceeds 60% and there is little or no air circulation, powdery mildew could form on your plant. Air circulation will help prevent that. This is just one example of how air circulation can help to prevent plant problems.

Let's address more air circulation components when using a fan in your grow environment. Make sure the fan oscillates. It is good for the fan to briefly blow directly onto the plant as that will help strengthen the plant's stems. However, the fan should not have constant wind blowing onto the plant because wind burn can occur. This is why an oscillating fan is key for ideal air circulation. It will allow air to blow on the plant briefly, then stop, then back onto the plant. This cycle is repeated over and over again, which mimics the wind in a natural environment. In turn, your plants will produce strong stems. Strong stems will be important as the plant goes into the flower stage. It will need strength to hold up those big beautiful buds that it produces. This can only happen with proper air circulation.

ENVIRONMENT

CO2

Carbon dioxide (CO2) is one of the most common gases on the earth. All humans and animals exhale carbon dioxide. CO2 is measured by parts per million (PPM). The carbon dioxide level that humans exhale is about 38,000 PPM. When a human exhales CO2, it's quickly mixed with the surrounding air.

Believe it or not, CO2 is essential for plant growth. Plants intake carbon dioxide in order to complete the process of photosynthesis. Indoor CO2 levels usually vary between 400-2,000 PPM while outdoor CO2 levels are usually in the range of 350-450 PPM. Outdoor CO2 levels are predominately controlled by gas exchange while indoor CO2 levels are mostly effected by human respiration. High levels of CO2 in a cannabis garden can result in stronger plants with increased yields – if introduced correctly.

When growing cannabis indoors, some growers supplement CO2 in their garden. Please note: depending on how many plants are being grown, CO2 supplementation is not required. Most indoor growers occupy the home or building they are growing in. Consequently, the CO2 that they exhale is enough for the plants. CO2 supplementation is more of an advanced technique; therefore, we will not cover it in detail in this beginner grow book.

ENVIRONMENT

Here are some notable CO2 PPM levels:

- 350-450 PPM – This is the range of the outdoor CO2 level.

- 1,000-1,500 PPM – This is the range that expert growers deem as the optimal level of CO2 for cannabis growth.

- 2,000 PPM - This level of CO2 is uncomfortable for humans. If in a grow environment with a PPM level this high, you will most likely become tired, drowsy, and/or encounter a headache.

Balancing TEMPERATURE & HUMIDITY

Balancing the temperature and humidity in your grow environment is much easier said than done. Back when I first started growing cannabis, I overlooked these crucial aspects and encountered extreme swings in temperature and humidity. Unfortunately, this led to my plants becoming so stressed that they became hermaphrodites. All of the plants in this particular instance produced both flowers and pollen sacs. My yield on that grow was significantly lower than my past grows. I certainly learned my lesson the difficult way by going through that experience. Hopefully, you can learn from my mistake.

There are multiple things that you can do to help balance the temperature and humidity in your grow environment. Below are some guidelines that you can refer to if you end up in a situation where you are struggling to keep those two conditions in their ideal ranges. The ideal ranges for temperature and humidity are specified in the temperature and humidity sections in this book.

If the temperature is too high, but the humidity is in the ideal range, slightly increase the speed of the inline fan. This will allow more hot air to exhaust out of the grow environment. If that does not reduce the temperature to the ideal range, add an air conditioner to the environment.

ENVIRONMENT

If the humidity is too high, but the temperature is in the ideal range, slightly increase the speed of the inline fan. This will allow more humidity to exhaust out of the grow environment. If that does not reduce the humidity to the ideal range, add a dehumidifier to the environment.

If both the temperature and humidity are too high, slightly increase the speed of the inline fan. This will allow more hot air and humidity to exhaust out of the grow environment. If that does not reduce the temperature and humidity to the ideal ranges, add an air conditioner and/or a dehumidifier to the environment.

If both the temperature and humidity are too low, slightly decrease the speed of the inline fan. This will allow hot air and humidity to stay in the environment. If that does not increase the temperature and humidity to the ideal ranges, add a heater and/or a humidifier to the environment.

Chapter 4
Vegetation

LIGHT CYCLE & DISTANCE

In order for a cannabis plant to grow, it needs light. It also needs a period of darkness each day. The plant light cycle refers to the cycle of light and darkness in which a plant receives. During the vegetation stage, I recommended an 18-6 light cycle. This means the grow light is on for 18 hours and it is off for 6 hours every single day. If you grow an autoflower plant, the light cycle will stay on 18-6 throughout the entire grow. Easy! If you are growing a photoperiod plant, the light cycle should be 18-6 for the vegetation stage only, and then it will change once the plant goes into the flower stage. We will cover the light cycle for the flower stage in the Flower chapter of this book.

Some growers prefer to do a 24-0 light cycle for the vegetation stage instead of an 18-6 light cycle. That means 24 hours of continuous light and zero hours of darkness. I have tried both the 24-0 light cycle and the 18-6 light cycle and did not see much of a difference in plant growth. Also, I certainly was not happy about the higher electricity bill that I received from keeping my grow lights on for 24 hours a day. Since there is not much of a difference between the two light cycles except the increase in electricity usage, I recommended the 18-6 light cycle for the vegetation stage.

Most growers automate the light cycle by using a timer. When your grow light is plugged into a timer, your light will automatically turn on or off according to the schedule you set on the timer. There are two main types of timers – digital and mechanical. Both types will work just fine. I personally use a digital timer since it is a little easier to program. The timer I use also has a backup battery so if there is a loss of electricity, the schedules I've set on the timer stay programmed. Incorporating a timer into your garden will prevent you from having to manually turn your grow light on and off each day.

When I talk about the light cycle, I have to address the light distance. This refers to the distance between the grow light and the top of the plant canopy. You do not want the grow light so close to the plant that the light burns the plant. For HID grow lights, I found that 20 to 36 inches away is usually a perfect distance in this stage. For LED grow lights, the recommended light distance is different for each grow light. The grow light manufacturer should have a recommendation for the light distance in the vegetation stage. Keep in mind that while the plants are in the vegetation stage, it is normal for you to have to adjust the grow light (move it farther away from the plants) everyday since the plants are growing so rapidly. That is where a set of adjustable light ratchets help make this job a little easier.

This HID grow light is too close to the seedlings. Since the grow light was too close, the seedlings burned and died.

WATERING

When it comes to water, cannabis plants are not very picky. Tap water from the faucet can be given to the plant and it should grow just fine. Be warned though, some municipal water systems put a high percentage of chlorine in their water. Chlorine could kill the beneficial bacteria in your growing medium. Tap water could also be considered hard water, which is when there is a high amount of minerals in the water. Watering the plant with hard water may or may not have negative effects on the cannabis plant. The extra minerals could actually be helpful for the plant; the plant will uptake them as extra nutrients. Conversely, the extra minerals in tap water could do harm on the plant instead. It all depends on what minerals are in the tap water, the amount of minerals, and if the cannabis plant can use them or not.

I use a reverse osmosis system. Reverse osmosis (RO) refers to water purification technology that remove ions, molecules, and larger particles from the water. RO water comes in at a 7.0 pH and once mixed with nutrients, will typically drop the pH. I talk more about pH in the next section of this book.

When should a cannabis plant be watered?

When growing cannabis in soil, the rule of thumb is to water when the soil is almost completely dry. To check this, simply stick your finger into the soil about an inch down. If the soil is dry the entire way, it is time for a watering. If the soil is still moist, do not give the plant water just yet. Too much water is bad for the plant. The plant will grow slower if it is drowning in water and too much water in the soil can also lead to pests such as fungus gnats.

Another method to determine if the plant needs to be watered is by checking the weight of the grow pot. Don't worry, you won't need to pull out the scale that you use to weigh yourself. You can simply lift the grow pot to get an idea if the growing medium still has water in it or not. This takes practice but with a little bit of experience you can judge the weight of the grow pot pretty accurately. Lift the grow pot when the medium is saturated with water to get a feel for the weight. Then lift the grow pot every day or two and you'll notice that the grow pot gets lighter and lighter as the plant uptakes the water from the medium. It typically takes about 2-4 days for soil to dry out after watering. Using both the finger-in-the-soil method and the weight method will help you determine when to water when growing in soil.

Coco coir, on the other hand, is an airier medium that holds less water. Due to this, it's difficult to over-water a cannabis plant growing in coco coir. A plant growing in coco coir will typically need to be watered every 1-2 days. Just like soil, you can stick your finger in the medium and also check the weight of the grow pot to determine if the plant needs water. The size of the plant and the size of the grow pot will also be a factor in how often you water.

How should a cannabis plant be watered?

The cannabis plant should be watered differently depending on what stage the plant is in. For example, if the plant has recently sprouted and is in the seedling stage on its first node, water by using a spray bottle to spray the plant and the medium around it. A node is the area of a plant's stem from which the leaves grow. Once the plant's second node has developed, water the plant by soaking the medium. Keep pouring water evenly into the medium until water comes out of the bottom of the grow pot. The water that comes out from the bottom of the grow pot is called the runoff. This is how you should water the plant for the rest of its life.

VEGETATION

PH

Monitoring the pH in the growing medium is one of the most important aspects of growing cannabis. It is also the most overlooked and is typically the root cause for many plant problems. pH is a measure of how acidic/basic water or a solution is. The range goes from 0 - 14, with 7 being neutral. A pH less than 7 indicate acidity, whereas a pH greater than 7 indicates a base.

> ## What is the right pH for a cannabis plant?

This varies depending on the growing medium that the cannabis plant is growing in. For soil, 6.0-7.0 pH is the right range. For hydroponic systems and soilless mediums such as coco coir, the right range is 5.5- 6.5 pH. If the pH goes out of that range, the plant could experience a nutrient lockout and then show signs of nutrient deficiencies. Even if there are nutrients in the medium, the plant cannot uptake them since the pH is not in the correct range.

How is pH measured and adjusted?

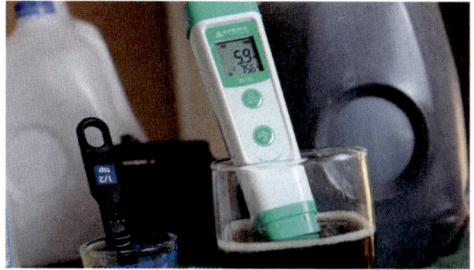

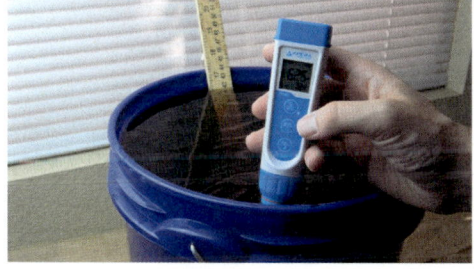

To measure the pH of your growing medium, you will need a tool such as a pH meter. There are pH test kits available, but those are not as accurate as a pH meter. To adjust the pH, there are solutions called pH Up and pH Down, which are sold online and at hydroponic shops. The process to check the pH will vary depending on the growing medium that the cannabis plant is in. When growing in soil, check and adjust the pH of the nutrient mix prior to feeding to the plant. Soil holds water and nutrients very well. Because of this, there will be a buffer. A buffer is a solution that resists changes in pH when combined with another solution of a different pH. Let me explain this using an example since it can be tricky to understand. If the soil runoff on a plant is 6.0 pH and you want to increase the pH to 6.5, then your nutrient solution should be above 6.5 pH. If you were to feed the plant a nutrient mix that is exactly 6.5 pH, it would probably only bring the medium up to 6.2-6.3 pH since there is a buffer. Therefore, in this example, feeding the plant a nutrient mix that is around 6.8 pH will help bring the pH up to the target of 6.5 pH.

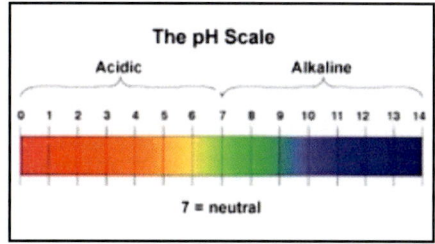

VEGETATION

Water the plant until water comes out of the bottom of the grow pot

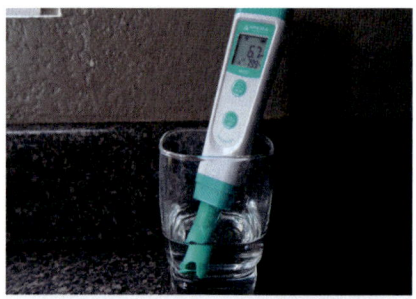

Scoop out a sample of water then test the pH of the water

The soil runoff is what you want to measure. First, feed or water the plant so that the solution runs all the way through the grow pot. Having a drip pan or saucer under the grow pot will help reduce a mess of water on the floor of your grow environment. Next, remove some of the water in the saucer. I like to use a small shot glass to scoop up some of the water in the saucer. Then, use a pH meter or pH test kit to identify the pH of the runoff. If growing in soil and the runoff pH is below 6.0, flush the plant. The flushing process is explained in detail in the Flushing section of this book. If the soil runoff pH is above 7.0, this typically means the plant needs nutrients. Check the PPM and feed the plant nutrients if needed. We talk in detail about PPM in the next section of this book.

When growing in coco coir, you also want to check and adjust the pH of the nutrient mix prior to feeding the plant. However, the runoff pH does not matter when growing in coco coir. Coco coir retains cations (positively charged ions). Consequently, the pH in the medium will change. I know, I promised that I wouldn't get into the science part of the plant. I'll stop there. Just know that the pH going into the medium is the only thing that matters when growing in coco coir. If you were to measure the pH of the runoff, the pH would most likely be higher than the pH of the nutrient mix that you put into the medium. Again, this is ok. The pH in coco coir will naturally increase. Since you only have to worry about the pH going into the medium, growing in coco coir is easier when it comes to ensuring the pH in your growing medium is in the right range.

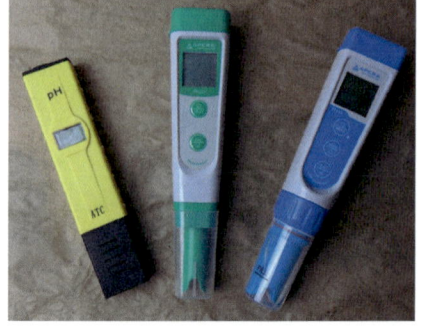

VEGETATION

PPM

Parts Per Million (PPM) is another measurement that should be monitored throughout the plant's life. Essentially, when growing cannabis, PPM is a measurement of the amount of nutrients present. In order to measure PPM, you will need a total dissolved solids (TDS) tester which is often referred to as a PPM meter and looks very similar to a pH meter. Whether growing cannabis in soil or coco coir, the runoff PPM is the most important. That measurement tells you how much nutrients are available in the medium for the plant's roots to uptake. It is also a good idea to measure the PPM of the water or nutrient mix you create prior to feeding the plant. This will help ensure you are giving the plant the right amount of nutrients. The PPM to target in the medium changes throughout the plant's life. When the plant is small, in the vegetation stage, the medium should have a low PPM since the plant is small and does not require much nutrients. As the plant grows and transitions into the flower stage, the plant will require more nutrients and therefore a higher PPM should be present in the medium.

Remember, the runoff measurement is the most important. The process of measuring the runoff to identify the PPM is similar to the process of measuring the pH. First, feed or water the plant so that the solution runs all the way through the grow pot. Having a drip pan or saucer under the grow pot will help reduce a mess of liquid on the floor of your grow environment. Next, remove some of the liquid in the saucer. I like to use a small shot glass to scoop up some of the liquid in the saucer. Then, place a TDS tester in the liquid to identify the PPM of the runoff.

VEGETATION

Here is a cheat sheet which shows the PPM range to target throughout the different stages of growth:

STAGE	TARGET PPM
After sprout, Vegetation week 1	100 to 250
Vegetation weeks 2-3	300 to 400
Vegetation weeks 4+	450 to 700
Flower weeks 1-4	750 to 950
Flower weeks 5+	1000 to 1600
Two weeks prior to harvest	less than 100

You may be wondering why two weeks prior to harvest the PPM to target in the medium is less than 100. The reason is because you want the least amount of nutrients present in the medium when you harvest the plant. Plants harvested with a high PPM left in the medium tend to result in bad tasting buds due to excessive chlorophyll being present. When those buds are then smoked, the smoker can experience a cutting, harsh feeling on the throat. Plants that are harvested with a low PPM left in the soil smoke better, taste better, and are less harsh on the throat.

Feeding
NUTRIENTS

Cannabis plants require many different nutrients in order to grow. As a beginner, you won't necessarily need to know every one of those nutrients. However, you should absolutely know the most common nutrients that the plant requires since feeding the plant too many or not enough of those nutrients can negatively impact the plant.
Here are the most common nutrients that cannabis plants need:

- Nitrogen- Nitrogen is key for both chlorophyll and protein production.
- Phosphorous- Phosphorous is used for energy transfer and storage. Also important in cell division, cell elongation, and root production.
- Potassium- Potassium helps strengthen the plant's immune system, which helps the plant cope with environmental stresses.
- Calcium- Calcium builds strong cell walls and a healthy root structure.
- Magnesium- Magnesium directly impacts the absorption of light processed and contributes to the creation of sugars and carbohydrates.

VEGETATION

If you feed the plant too many nutrients, the plant could encounter a nutrient lockout. The plant will show signs of nutrient burn, overall growth will slow down, and flower development will suffer. If you do not feed your plant enough nutrients, the plant will show signs of deficiencies, growth will slow down, flower development will slow down, and leaves will die off. In order to prevent nutrient lockout and deficiencies, make sure the pH and PPM in the growing medium are in the proper ranges.

When should nutrients be fed to a cannabis plant?

This depends on what growing medium you are using. Plants growing in coco coir will need to be fed earlier (and more often) than plants growing in soil. Let's first talk about when nutrients should be fed to a cannabis plant growing in soil.

If you are using a soil that does not have nutrients in it or a very low amount of nutrients, feed shortly after the plant sprouts from the soil. If you are using a soil that already has nutrients in it such as FoxFarm Ocean Forest soil, the first feeding should be around day 20-40 after the plant sprouts. Although, it may be even longer than that if you transplant the plant into a larger container. Every time you transplant the plant, the fresh soil that goes into the container has nutrients in it so you don't need to feed the plant bottled nutrient just yet. Because of this, it can be hard to determine when to start feeding the plant bottled nutrients. You can get a more accurate answer by checking the PPM of the soil runoff as that will tell you how much nutrients are present in the soil. Then, simply use the cheat sheet in the PPM section of this book to identify how much nutrients to give to the plant.

VEGETATION

This plant has a significant calcium deficiency since the grower did not use CalMag

This plant was fed too much nitrogen which has resulted in nitrogen toxicity

This plant was not fed enough phosphorus

When growing cannabis in soil, you should not feed the plant nutrients every time the grow pot dries out. Soil tends to hold nutrients longer compared to other growing mediums, therefore, use the water-feed-water-feed technique. This technique consists of first watering the plant by following the instructions in the Watering section of this book. Next, when the grow pot dries out, feed the plant nutrients. You would then repeat so every other time the grow pot dries out, the plant is only receiving plain water.

When growing cannabis in coco coir, begin feeding the plant nutrients immediately after the plant sprouts. Coco coir is an airy medium and therefore doesn't hold as much water and nutrients. As a result, the medium dries out quicker and you will need to feed the plant nutrients every time the medium dries out instead of every-other time like when growing in soil. Depending on the plant's root structure and the size of the grow pot, it's common to feed plants growing in coco coir every 24-48 hours. Warning! Even though coco coir doesn't hold nutrients as well as soil does, nutrients may build up in the medium.

Always check the PPM of the runoff. If the PPM is above the ideal range according the cheat sheet in the PPM section of this book, give the plant plain water instead of nutrients. However, this scenario may not occur. That's one of the reasons why it's so important to monitor the PPM of the runoff.

What nutrients should be fed to a cannabis plant?

At the minimum, cannabis plants should be fed base nutrients. Base nutrients consist of various levels of nitrogen, phosphorus, potassium, calcium, magnesium, iron, manganese, zinc, sulfur, and several other minor elements. Most nutrient companies have either a 2-part or 3-part series of base nutrients which consists of 2 or 3 bottles respectively. Those bottles should come with feeding instructions. Keep in mind that most companies formulate their nutrients for a wide variety of plants and that a full dose according to their feeding chart is too much for cannabis plants. Therefore, I recommend you start with a ½ or ¼ doses of nutrients. Measure the PPM of the nutrient mix prior to feeding the plant to ensure you aren't giving the plant too heavy of a feeding.

If you are growing in coco coir or growing with a LED grow light, you will most likely need an additive called CalMag in addition to base nutrients. CalMag consists of calcium, magnesium, and often times nitrogen as well. When growing in coco coir or a soil that isn't precharged with nutrients, feed the plant CalMag after the plant sprouts. If growing in a soil that already has nutrients in it, you probably won't need to feed the plant CalMag until the plant uses up the nutrients in the soil. Follow the feeding schedule on the bottle of CalMag. Often times, especially when growing in coco coir, if a plant is given a half dose of CalMag according to the instructions on the bottle, it isn't enough. If this occurs, the plant will show calcium deficiency, magnesium deficiency, or both.

There are several other additives that can be fed to cannabis plants. A few of the most common are silica, bloom boosters, and microbial inoculates (often called microbes). These additives aren't required or recommended for beginners, and therefore, we won't go over them in detail in this book.

What order should nutrients be mixed?

In order to prevent nutrients from binding together, resulting in the plant's inability to uptake them, nutrients should be mixed in water instead of mixed together. Additionally, the nutrients should be added to the water in a specific order. Make sure to stir or shake the mixture after each nutrient is added to the water. Here is the order that the nutrients should be added to the water:

1. Silica
2. CalMag
3. Base Nutrients
4. Additives
5. PH Up/Down
6. Microbial Inoculants

Remember to monitor the pH and the PPM. If the PPM of the runoff is above the range recommended in the PPM section of this book, give the plant plain water instead of nutrients. Look at the plant to see if anything does not look right. If the leaves look too dark or too light, skip to the last chapter of this book in order to identify the problem. Most of the time, discoloration issues (too dark or too light) means that you are feeding the plant too many nutrients or not enough.

WEEKS 1-2

The first two weeks after the plant sprouts is often referred to as the seedling stage. It can be exciting to see your plant grow its first set of leaves...but growth may seem slow. The plant is not going to grow a whole lot of height and you may even be worried that something is wrong. Be patient. During this time period, the plant is mostly growing its root structure. Roots grow deep down into the medium and reach for the bottom of the grow pot looking for more water. The larger the root structure, the easier it will be to intake enough water and nutrients to support the growth of a large plant.

As the plant grows, you must move the light higher so the temperature at canopy level is in the 70-85°F/21-30°C range. The humidity should be in the 65-85% range. If you are using a HID grow light, use the MH bulb during these weeks. Dial the ballast down to the lowest setting (150-250w). If you are using a LED grow light, adjust the light so the distance from the top of the plant is what the manufacturer recommends. Many LED grow lights have a switch for the vegetation stage (Veg) and a switch for the flower stage (Bloom). Use the Veg switch only during these first few weeks (if applicable).

VEGETATION

Do not let the medium dry out! If you soaked the medium prior to planting the seed, the medium could stay moist for around a week, however, it may dry out quicker depending on your grow environment. Keep the top of the medium moist at all times. Use a spray bottle to spray water onto the top of the medium. Depending on the type of medium you are using, you may only need to soak the medium once or twice during these first few weeks of the plant's life.

Place a fan inside your grow environment to ensure proper air circulation. Air circulation is important throughout all stages of the plant's life. Be aware of the strength of the air movement while the plant is a seedling. I recommend turning the fan's oscillating feature off (if applicable) and positioning the fan to blow away from the plant instead of directly onto the plant. If the fan is blowing directly onto the plant, the plant may encounter wind burn which will result in a stunt in growth. Ideally, the fan is placed so the air movement causes the plant to slightly sway. This will replicate the wind in an outdoor environment and will help the plant develop a strong stalk.

CHEAT SHEET - SEEDLING/VEGETATION WEEKS 1-2	
Temperature (at canopy level)	70-80°F/21-27°C (HID)
	75-85°F/24-30°C (LED)
Humidity	65-85%
Light cycle	Light cycle 18-6 (18 hours on, 6 hours off)
Light distance (from top of canopy)	Approximately 36" (HID)
	Contact light manufacturer (LED)

VEGETATION

WEEKS 3+

Weeks 3 and beyond in the vegetation stage is what I like to call the explosive growth period. If the plant is healthy, it is normal for the plant to grow inches overnight! You will notice that the medium dries out faster and that's because the root structure is now bigger and can uptake more water and nutrients. Follow the PPM cheat sheet located in the PPM section of this book and feed the plant nutrients as needed to keep the PPM in the ideal range.

As the plant grows, continue to move the light higher and target the canopy-level temperature to be in the 70-85°F/21-30°C range. The humidity should be lowered down to the 45-65% range. If you are using a HID grow light, keep the MH bulb in during these weeks. The ballast can now be turned up to the maximum setting. If you are using a LED grow light, adjust the light so the distance from the top of the plant is what the manufacturer recommends. You can continue to use the Veg switch during this time period, but many growers will also turn on the Bloom switch so the plant receives a full light spectrum.

The plant should be large enough at this point so it can encounter direct air movement from a fan without harming it. Therefore, turn on the fan's oscillating feature (if applicable). The air movement should cause the plants to sway, which again, will help strengthen the branches. This is the type of movement you should target for the remainder of the plant's life.

If the plant is in a small container, the plant will need to be transplanted into a larger container during these weeks. If you plan to do low-stress training (LST), topping, or pruning, now is the perfect time to do it. We go over transplanting, LST, topping, and pruning in detail in the next four sections of this book.

You can keep a photoperiod plant in the vegetation stage as long as you desire. The plant will simply keep growing and growing until the light cycle is changed, which we will cover in the Flower chapter. Keep in mind that once the light cycle is changed, the plant will stretch for the first 2-3 weeks of the flower stage. The plant could stretch to nearly double its size, so do not keep the plant in the vegetation stage too long or else you may run into height issues while in the flower stage.

CHEAT SHEET - VEGETATION WEEKS 3+	
Temperature (at canopy level)	70-80°F/21-27°C (HID)
	75-85°F/24-30°C (LED)
Humidity	45-65%
Light cycle	18-6 (18 hours on, 6 hours off)
Light distance (from top of canopy)	24-36" (HID)
	Contact light manufacturer (LED)

*Trans*PLANTING

Depending on the size container that you planted your cannabis seed into, you may need to transplant the plant one or more times in its life. Transplanting is the process of moving the plant from one container to another – typically into a larger container. The transplanting process should be done in the vegetation stage only since this process sometimes shocks the plant, which can stunt its growth. This is called transplant shock. If a plant is transplanted while in the flower stage, and the plant encounters transplant shock, yield will suffer.

If you are growing an autoflower plant, you should have planted the seed directly into a 3, 4, or 5-gallon grow pot. I do not recommend transplanting autoflower plants. Autoflowers automatically go into the flower stage without the changing of a light cycle. Therefore, if transplant shock were to occur, the plant may not have enough time to recover prior to flowering and yield could be negatively impacted.

With photoperiod plants, transplanting can be done during the vegetation stage without the fear of transplant shock impacting yield. The light cycle is controlled so if transplant shock were to occur, the plant can be kept in the vegetation stage until the plant fully recovers. Then, the light cycle can be switched to flowering. I talk more about switching the light cycle for photoperiod plants in the Flower chapter.

" When should a plant be transplanted? "

Transplant the plant from the initial small container into a 1-gallon grow pot when the plant has developed at least its second node. Some growers prefer to wait until the plant has developed its 3rd or even 4th node to ensure the plant has a large enough root structure. Approximately 7-14 days later, the plant should have doubled its height and should then be transplanted again into its final container – a 3, 4, or 5-gallon grow pot.

Steps to transplant:

1. Fill the new grow pot 3/4 of the way full with the growing medium.
2. Dig a hole in the middle of the new grow pot to make room for the plant.
2a. (optional) Place the old container into the center of the new container and surround the new container with medium.
2b. (optional) Remove the old container which reveals a perfectly shaped hole for your plant.
2c. (optional) Sprinkle some mycorrhizae into the hole which will help prevent transplant shock.
3. Loosen the plant by gently squeezing the grow pot on all sides.
4. Remove the plant from its current grow pot. The plant and medium should be held together by the roots.
5. Place the plant in the hole in the new grow pot.
6. Put more medium into the grow pot but leave an inch or two of space from the top of the grow pot. This helps prevent overflow when watering.
7. Lightly pack down the medium.
8. Water the plant if growing in soil that has nutrients. Feed the plant if growing in coco coir or a soil without nutrients in it.

VEGETATION

Fill the new container with soil

Remove the plant from the current container and place into new container

Fill the new container with soil

VEGETATION

Low-Stress Training (LST)

Low-stress training (LST) is the method of bending and tying down the branches of a plant. The goal is for side branches to then grow upward to create an even canopy. The canopy is the uppermost layer of the plant. If you choose not to do LST, the plant will grow straight up and one branch will form a main cola. A cola refers to a cluster of buds that grow tightly together. The plant will then focus most of its energy producing buds on that one cola while the other branches will not grow as many buds.

As branches are being tied down, other branches are growing upwards which will result in multiple branches fighting to become the main cola. If the canopy is even, this will also allow light to be evenly distributed onto the plant. The more branches shooting up towards the light, the more colas will grow. This will result in a higher yield. LST is an optional process. I was not sure if I wanted to include low-stress training in this book or not, but decided to. Even though the process is optional, you may need to do LST if you have height restrictions in your grow environment.

VEGETATION

When should LST be performed?

I recommend you start LST when the plant has grown to at least the fifth node.

LST Steps:

1. Bend down and tie the plant to the side of the grow pot. Do not use anything sharp such as string to tie down the plant. Instead, use soft ties or twisty ties.

First step of LST - tie the plant to the side of the container

2. Once the other branches have grown up, tie them down to different sides of the grow pot.

3. Adjust the ties as necessary to maintain an even canopy. It's normal to adjust the ties every day or two depending on growth.

Plant is attached to the grow pot using a clip

4. Continue to tie down branches to allow other branches to grow and reach the same height. The more branches shooting up towards the light, the higher yield you will get. I personally target 8 to 16 branches per plant.

Plant with LST in flowering

5. Once the desired number of branches have grown to the height you want and the canopy is even, switch the light cycle to force flowering. We talk about how to force the plant into flowering in the next chapter.

Untrained plant with one main cola

Trained plant with multiple colas

TOPPING

Topping is a high-stress training technique where the top of the plant is cut between its nodes. This will result in the growth of two main colas instead of just one. Like LST, this process is optional, but it will certainly help increase yield if done correctly.

If you are growing an autoflower plant, I do not recommend topping the plant. Topping will slow down the growth of the plant. Since autoflowers automatically flower at or around day 30, any negative impact to growth will lower the yield. If you are growing a photoperiod plant, the topping process should be done in the vegetation stage only. A photoperiod plant will then be able to recover from the topping process before flowering. Since the plant isn't flowering just yet, yield will not be negatively impacted. If a plant is topped while in the flower stage, flower development will stop until the plant has recovered. This will result in a lower yield.

There are many different topping strategies. I personally like to top my plant when it has just developed its fifth node. Once the fifth node appears, I top the plant down to its third node. I also remove the growth at the first node but leave the growth at the second node. From there, I wait until the branches have developed their third node and will top again down to their second node on those branches. During this process, I also perform LST in order to maintain an even canopy. Again, there are many different topping strategies. Feel free to experiment as you wish.

VEGETATION

PRUNING

Pruning (often called lollipopping) is another optional plant training technique which is done in an attempt to increase yield. Pruning is the process of cutting off branches and leaves on the plant. Some growers will also prune their plant to increase airflow on the lower part of the plant. They do this as a preventative measure to reduce the chances of powdery mildew forming on the plant.

When a plant grows naturally without pruning, the plant focuses its energy on developing branches and leaves throughout the entire plant. Unfortunately, this can lead to the lower third of the plant to have underdeveloped bud sites. Consequently, since the plant is focusing its attention on those underdeveloped areas, the top buds are not growing as big as they could be. This is when pruning becomes beneficial. Pruning will help a plant to re-focus its energy on what matters most – top bud development.

I recommend pruning the bottom third of the plant only. To prune, simply use scissors or trimmers to snip away all leaves on the bottom third of the plant. Make sure to first wipe down the scissors with isopropyl alcohol. This will help prevent the plant from getting infected. Next, remove any small branches on the bottom third of the plant that has not grown at least ½ the size of the plant. Ultimately, if that branch is not seeing any light then it will not develop big buds - just remove it.

VEGETATION

Pruning should take place either late in the vegetation stage (just before changing the light schedule) or within the first two weeks of the flower stage. The reason for this is because removing branches or leaves ultimately hurts the plant and will slightly stunt its growth. If you prune after the second week in the flower stage, then the plant will focus on repairing itself first instead of focusing on creating buds – resulting in a lower yield.

Keep in mind that pruning is completely optional. Feel free to either prune so the plant focuses its energy on top-bud development or let the plant grow naturally.

Pruned the lower third of the plant

Chapter 5
Flower

FORCING FLOWERING

The flower stage often proves to be an exciting stage for growers as this is when the plant will start to produce flowers – often referred to as buds. In a previous chapter, we talked about how autoflower plants will automatically flower. Remember, those plants should stay on an 18-6 light cycle for the entire grow. Photoperiod plants, on the other hand, will need to be forced into the flower stage. Flowering is forced by simply changing the light cycle. Photoperiod cannabis plants will not start to flower until the light cycle changes. Once the light cycle changes, the flowering stage officially begins.

What light cycle will force flowering?

In order to force flowering, change the light cycle to 12-12, which means 12 hours with the grow light on and 12 hours with the grow light off. When the grow light is off, your grow tent or grow room should be completely dark. Light leaking onto your plant during its dark period could cause the plant to become a hermaphrodite. Keep the plant on a 12-12 light cycle until harvest. The first day that the plant receives 12 hours of light, that counts as day 1 of the flowering stage.

SEXING

Cannabis plants can be either male or female. Female plants produce flowers and male plants produce pollen sacs. Male cannabis plants are essentially worthless to most growers. If the plant turns out to be a male, you are probably going to want to kill that plant as quickly as possible unless you plan to breed with it. If you keep the male plant in the same environment as a female plant, the male plant will release pollen onto the female plant and the female plant will produce seeds inside its buds.

You will see signs of sex either around week six while the plant is in the vegetation stage, or around weeks 1-2 after the light cycle is changed to 12-12. If you planted Feminized seeds, then the plant will automatically be female. If you planted regular seeds, you can expect about 50% of the plants to be male and the other 50% of the plants to be female.

> How can a male and a female plant be identified?

If the plant is female, it will produce pistils. If the plant is male, it will produce pollen sacs. Both pistils and pollen sacs form at the nodes of the plant. Some growers mistake the plant's stipules for pistils. A stipule is a small leaf-like appendage to a leaf, typically borne in pairs at the base of the leaf stalk. Stipules form on both male and female plants.

A plant that is female will have pistils

A plant that is male will form pollen sacs.
Do not confuse the plant's stipules for pistils.

WEEKS 1-3

The first three weeks of the flower stage is often referred to as the stretching phase. You should expect significant growth during this period. The sex of the plant will be determined (if you haven't already) during this phase. One important aspect to note is that the plant will still grow upwards for the first 2-3 weeks in the flower stage. During this phase, the plant could potentially double in height. If you think the plant will grow taller than the height of your grow space, you may want to top the plant or perform LST.

During this stage, the plant now focuses its energy on producing flowers. Monitor the plant closely and look for signs of problems such as pests and deficiencies. Depending on the grow pot size, you will probably need to feed or water the plant every 2-3 days - if not every day. Feeding the plant nutrients during this stage is critical due to the plant's rapid growth. Refer the Feeding Nutrients section of this book for more details on how to feed your plant.

In the first few weeks of the stretching phase, the humidity should be in the 40-55% range. If using HID lighting, the HPS bulb should be used and the ballast should be on the highest setting. Move the grow light higher or lower so the temperature at canopy level is in the 70-80°F/21-27°C range but not so low that the plant is burned.

FLOWER

If using LED lighting, keep the temperature in the 75-85°F/24-30°C range. If your LED grow light has a switch for Veg and a switch for Bloom, turn both switches on for this stage. If you want the plant to produce the biggest buds possible, all of these factors need to be adhered to and monitored during these weeks.

CHEAT SHEET - FLOWER WEEKS 1-3	
Temperature (at canopy level)	70-80°F/21-27°C (HID)
	75-85°F/24-30°C (LED)
Humidity	40-55%
Light cycle (photoperiod plants)	12-12 (12 hours on, 12 hours off)
Light cycle (autoflower plants)	18-6 (18 hours on, 6 hours off)
Light distance (from top of canopy)	Approximately 12-24" (HID)
	Contact light manufacturer (LED)

WEEKS 4+

For weeks four and beyond in the flower stage, the plant is done growing upwards. This is the time the plant now focuses its energy on producing buds. Keep in mind that most strains should be in the flower stage for 8-10 weeks before being harvested. Contact the seed bank or breeder if you are unsure of how long the strain that you are growing should be in the flower stage.

Continue to feed the plant nutrients during these weeks. Depending on what nutrients are being used, the plant will probably need more than a ¼ dose of nutrients during feeding. A ½ dose or even a full dose of nutrients during feeding is typically what the plant needs during these weeks. Monitor the plant closely and look for signs of problems such as pests and deficiencies.

If using HID lighting, the HPS bulb should be used and the ballast should be on the highest setting. This is the same as in weeks 1-3 of the flowering stage. If using an LED grow light, both the Veg and Bloom switches should be on for this stage (if available). The temperature at canopy level should now be in the 65-80°F/18-27°C range. Notice how up to this point I recommended 70-85°F/21-30°C temperature range for the plant. Now, the ideal temperature should drop into the high 60°F/16°C. This indoor temperature drop replicates nature's fall season outside.

Keep the humidity in the 30-50% range. Again, notice the drop in the recommended humidity compared to previous weeks. If there is high humidity in the grow environment during these weeks, the plant is at risk of bud rot and mold developing, which can completely wipe out the entire crop. Accordingly, it is imperative that the humidity is kept lower than 60% for the remainder of the grow.

For the last two weeks of the grow, flush the plant and give the plant nothing but water. Refer to the Flushing section in this book to learn how to flush. Do not feed the plant nutrients during the last two weeks of the grow. If the plant is fed nutrients all the way up to the harvest, the finished buds will have a horrible taste and will be harsh on the throat when smoked due to the amount of chlorophyll present. Keep the humidity as low as possible for these last two weeks. This will be another indication to the plant that its life is near the end. Consequently, the plant will continue to produce as many buds as possible until the harvest.

> ## How can I determine when the plant is two weeks before harvest?

A microscope can be used to look at the plant's trichomes to determine readiness. Learn more about this in the Harvesting section of this book.

FLOWER

CHEAT SHEET - FLOWER WEEKS 4+

Temperature (at canopy level)	65-80°F/18-27°C
Humidity	30-50%
Light cycle (photoperiod plants)	12-12 (12 hours on, 12 hours off)
Light cycle (autoflower plants)	18-6 (18 hours on, 6 hours off)
Light distance (from top of canopy)	Approximately 12-24" (HID)
	Contact light manufacturer (LED)

FLOWER

FLUSHING

Flushing is the process of running a large amount water through the medium and letting it drain out of the bottom of the grow pot. This is done to reduce the amount of nutrients in the medium. If you've used synthetic nutrients during your grow, you should flush your plant prior to harvest in order improve the taste and smoke of your buds. You may also need to flush your plant during your grow if you run into problems such as too high of parts per million (PPM) or a toxicity issue.

> How much water should be used to flush the plant?

The rule of thumb is to take the size grow pot (in gallons) and double that number. For example, if the plant is in a 3-gallon grow pot, run six gallons of water through the medium. If the plant is in a 5-gallon grow pot, run 10 gallons of water through the medium. Most home growers will put their plant in their bathtub and run water through it that way. Other growers choose to use a wet vacuum such as a shop vac to vacuum the water from the grow pot saucer. The choice is yours.

Use a PPM meter to monitor the PPM of the runoff. If you are flushing mid-grow, refer to the cheat sheet in the PPM section in this book to identify the appropriate PPM range for your plant. If you are flushing the plant prior to harvest, typically aim to reduce the runoff PPM to around 100. A PPM of 100 will aid in achieving the best tasting buds.

Depending on how many nutrients are in the medium, you may need to run more or less water through the medium than advised above with the "doubling the gallons according to the size of the grow pot" guidance. Some growers will flush their plant multiple times during the last few weeks of the plant's life in order to achieve the goal of around 100 PPM. Others will simply flush their plant once to get the PPM down around 100 and will then give their plant water for the remainder of its life as needed when the grow pot dries out. Either way is acceptable.

Since the medium will not have many nutrients in it during the two weeks prior to harvest, most of the plant's leaves should change color from green to yellow. This is perfectly fine. The plant knows the end of its life is coming and is using up the little bit of nutrients still left in the plant and medium to ripen its buds.

Chapter 6
Harvest

HARVESTING

You spent months caring for the plant and watched it grow from seed into a bountiful plant. Harvesting can be a sad time for some, since cutting the plant down is technically killing it. You will probably get over that feeling quickly as you are overcome with a feeling of accomplishment. You did it! You successfully grew cannabis and can now move onto the final processes which consist of harvesting, trimming, drying, and curing.

> When should a cannabis plant be harvested?

The old-school method of determining when to harvest a cannabis plant is to simply look at the plant and harvest when all the plant's pistils have turned from white to orange. This method is still in use today, but not by many growers since there is a better way.

The newer, more accurate method, is by looking at the trichomes on the plant's buds and then harvesting when they reach a certain stage. Trichomes are small resin glands present on the flowers and leaves of the plant and are often referred to as "frost" by many growers. It is within the head of the trichome that the actual production of cannabinoids like THC occurs. The trichomes can be seen with a naked eye but a handheld microscope is needed to see them up close and what stage they are in. There are 3 different stages for trichomes:

Clear trichomes

Amber trichomes

Cloudy trichomes

- Clear - If the plant's trichomes are 75% or more clear, then the plant is not ready for harvest. Clear trichomes are underdeveloped and the plant still has energy to create more buds and more trichomes. If the plant is harvested at this point, the high felt after smoking weed with clear trichomes may be too energetic resulting in anxiety. Also, the high may not last very long.

- Cloudy - When the trichome heads mostly appear cloudy or milky in color, one will typically experience a more heady, energetic, and sativa-like high. The trichomes are fully developed and are at their highest potency. Therefore, most growers like to harvest their plant when the trichomes are in this stage.

- Amber – If most of the trichomes on the plant are an amber color, a more relaxed body high that's stereotypically associated with indica strains will be felt. Amber trichomes are over-developed and the THC within the trichomes have converted from THC to CBN. This is actually a degradation in potency. I rarely hear about growers harvesting their plant when all the trichomes are amber. Instead, many growers harvest when most trichomes are amber and the rest are cloudy.

How do I harvest the plant?

Once the trichomes are at the stage you desire, the plant can now be harvested. Harvesting cannabis simply consists of cutting down the plant, and then the trim, dry, and cure processes. The plant can be harvested by either cutting individual branches of the plant or by cutting the main stem of the plant by the base.

TRIMMING

Trimming is the process of cutting off the leaves and stems of the plant so only buds remain. After the plant is harvested, you can either trim the plant or let the plant go through the drying process first. If the plant is trimmed before the plant is dry, this is called a wet trim. If the plant is trimmed after the plant has completed the drying process, this is called a dry trim.

> When should a wet trim be done vs a dry trim?

This is totally up to you. After the plant is cut down, there is still water in the branches and buds. If the plant is hung to dry without trimming off the leaves or cutting up the branches, the plant will dry slower. This can be good if you live in environment that has low humidity. If the plant dries too fast then it could lead to over-drying which will result in the buds being harsh in the throat when smoked.

If the environment is typically normal to high humidity, then you may want to trim the leaves off and cut up the branches before drying. Removing the leaves and cutting up the branches will help speed up the drying process which can be good for normal to high-humid environments.

The trimming process is extremely time consuming and therefore some call it "trim jail." Depending on the size of the plant, it is normal to spend 2-4 hours to trim just one medium-sized plant. I figured I would give you that figure so you can plan your time accordingly for the trimming process. Now that you have a timeframe for trimming, let's discuss the actual trimming process.

To trim, a normal pair of scissors can be used, but I highly suggest using hand pruners instead. Hand pruners have a spring to automatically open up the blades so only the motion of squeezing the hand to close the blades need to be performed. This may not sound like a big deal, but remember, trimming takes several hours and the repetitive motion does put strain on the hand. Using hand pruners will in fact reduce that strain.

Before trimming

After trimming

HARVEST

Here are some guidelines on how to trim a cannabis plant:

- Holding one branch at a time, cut the leaves off the branch so only the buds are attached to the branch.

- When cutting off the leaves, cut as much of each leaf's stem off as well.

- For the leaves where the stem is buried between buds, do not break apart buds in order to try to reach the stem of the leaf. Simply cut off as much of the leaf as you can.

- After all the leaves are cut from the branch, cut the stems of the buds to separate from the branch, then dispose of the branch.

- Trimmed leaves can be used to make things such as hash and butter or can simply be disposed.

Before trimming a leaf from the base of the stem

After removing the trimmed leaf

The stems of the leaves are buried between the buds

Cutting off most of the leaf

DRYING

After the plant is cut down, the branches and buds will still have water in them. They need to be dry before going into the curing process. If done correctly, the drying process typically takes about 7-10 days. The first step is to hang the plant upside down. Most growers use clothes hangers and wooden clothes pins to do this. The entire plant can be hung, or the branches can be cut from the main stem and then hung individually.

In order to prevent the plant from over-drying or worse, mold appearing on the buds, the humidity should be between 55-60% and the temperature should be around 70°F/21°C. The environment should be dark since light degrades the THC in the trichomes. Since controlling the humidity during the drying process can be difficult for beginners, some growers will use an empty grow tent as the place to dry their plant. A humidifier and/or dehumidifier can be used to help get the humidity in the environment between 55-60%.

A fan should also be placed in the drying environment so that air circulates. This will help prevent humid spots and will reduce the chances of mold appearing on the buds. However, make sure that the fan is not blowing directly onto the buds. If the fan is blowing directly onto the buds, then the buds may dry too quickly or some may dry faster than others.

There are two methods you can use to determine if the plant is ready to be cured – by squeezing the buds and by snapping the stems. If you squeeze the buds and they still feel moist, then they need to dry longer. If once the buds are squeezed and they feel dry, then they are ready to move onto the curing process. The stems can also be used to determine if the plant is dry. If the stem cleanly snaps when bent, then the plant is ready for curing. If the stem does not cleanly snap when bent, then water is still in it. At that point, the buds still have water in them so keep them in the drying process longer before moving onto the curing process.

CURING

Curing is the last step in the process before the buds are able to be smoked. Curing is simply the method of preserving. Essentially, even after completing the drying process in the previous section, the buds will still have moisture inside of them. Curing will slowly bring that moisture out from the middle of the buds. The target is for the humidity of the buds to be around 62% in order to achieve the smoothest smoke. Also, the curing process will break down chlorophyll to significantly improve taste, get rid of the "cut grass" smell the buds have, will reduce harshness when smoked, and will result in better tasting buds.

Sure, you can skip the curing process and smoke the buds right away. But be warned, the taste will be horrible and very harsh on your throat.

Here is what is needed for the curing process:

- Mason jar(s) – A 32 oz. wide-mouth jar will fit around an ounce of weed. A wide-mouth jar will make putting buds in the jar and taking them out easier than a regular mason jar.

- Hygrometer – This will show what the humidity is inside the jar.

- Boveda 62 humidity pack – This humidity pack will increase / decrease the humidity in the container so it settles at 62% - the perfect humidity for your buds to be stored in.

If you have not done it already, cut the buds from their branches. Put the buds and a hygrometer in a mason jar, but be sure to leave about 1-2 inches of space left in the jar. Close the jar and wait 30 minutes. After the buds sit in the jar for 30 minutes, take a look at the hygrometer in the jar.

If the hygrometer shows:

- Above 70% – The buds are at risk for mold! Remove the buds from jar and place on something such as a piece of paper or cardboard for 1-2 hours, then place back in the jar.

- 65-70% – Remove the lid of jar but leave the buds in the jar. Wait 15-30 minutes. Shake the jar. If the buds stick together when shaking, that means they are too moist. Take them out of the jar for about 30 minutes to an hour.

- 60-65% – Cure zone! This is the ideal range for the buds to be in. 62% is the best.

- Less than 60% – Too dry. Put a humidity pack in the jar with the buds in an attempt to re-hydrate them.

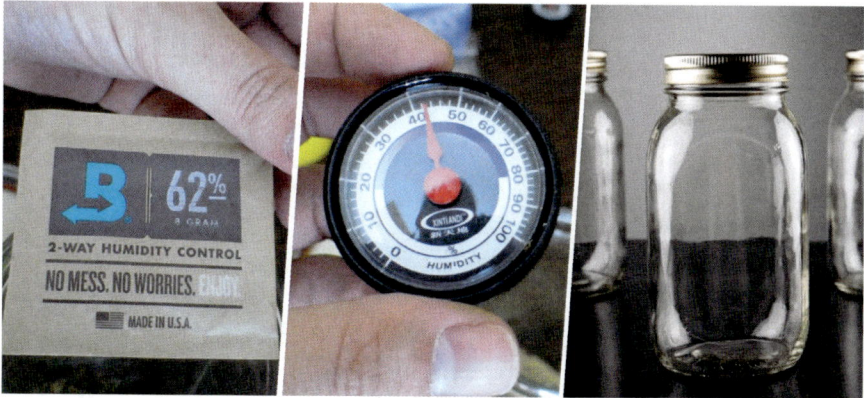

Keep the jar in a dark place that is around room temperature (70°F/21°C). Check on the jar every few hours and make adjustments as listed on the previous page.

"Burp" the jars at least once a day. Burping is simply removing the lid of the jar for about a minute and shaking the buds while in the jar. Remember, if the buds stick together, that means they are too moist and should be taken out of the jar for about 30 minutes to an hour.

Once the jar is stable between 60-65% RH, place the Boveda 62 humidity pack inside the jar with the buds. The humidity pack will lower or increase the humidity and will become stable at 62%. Still burp the jar once a day.

After the buds are stable at 62% humidity for 2-4 weeks, the jar no longer needs to be burped daily. If the jar is being stored long-term, I recommend to still burp the jars once a month. The buds can be stored like this for several years without worry!

Congratulations! You did it! You completed the entire grow process from seed to smoke!

Chapter 7
Problems

PROBLEMS

I hope you never have to read this chapter. That statement probably sounds strange coming from the author, huh? This chapter's sole purpose is to give you solutions to problems you could encounter when growing cannabis indoors. Sure, the plant could grow and have zero issues. It is possible. I hope that is the case for you. However, many new growers do face problems during their first attempt at growing. Most problems can be corrected – as long as the problem is caught and fixed quickly. Other problems could result in the plant becoming so contaminated that it needs to be killed. In this chapter, I cover the top 12 most common problems that you may face while growing cannabis indoors.

Calcium deficiency

Nitrogen and phosphorus deficiency

PROBLEMS

pH
FLUCTUATIONS

DESCRIPTION: In order for a plant to take up nutrients through its roots, the pH of the soil needs to be managed. When growing cannabis in soil, the pH of the medium should be between 6.0-7.0. When growing in coco coir, the pH of the medium should be between 5.5-6.5. If the pH fluctuates outside the proper range, the plant could become stressed and brown or tan spots could appear on some leaves. If left untreated, the plant could also encounter nutrient lockout and other signs of deficiencies could surface.

PROBLEM: Some leaves on the middle or lower parts of the plant show tan or brown spotting.

SOLUTION(S): Measure the pH of the runoff. If growing in soil and the pH is below 6.0, water the plant with a 6.8 pH solution. If the soil runoff pH is above 8.0, water the plant with a 6.2 pH solution. If growing in coco coir and the pH is outside the range of 5.5-6.5, water the plant with a 5.8 pH solution.

Heat Stress & LIGHT BURN

DESCRIPTION: High heat or too much light can stress out the plant.

PROBLEM: When the temperature is too high, the plant's leaves will curl upwards like a taco. When there is too much light, leaves will turn yellow, or brown spotting may appear on impacted areas. The yellowing and brown spotting of leaves will most likely appear on the top of the plant which is closest to the light. You may also see light bleaching which is a form of light burn. This is when the top of the buds closest to the light appear white.

SOLUTION(S): Heat stress

> Make sure the temperature/humidity monitor is placed at canopy level. Canopy level temperature should be between 70-85°F/21-30°C throughout the entire grow (except the last few weeks of the flower stage when dropping into the 60°F/16°C range benefits the plant). Move the light up if the canopy-level temperature is too high.

PROBLEMS

- Position the oscillating fan in the grow environment that so air circulates throughout the entire environment. This will prevent hot and humid spots from forming.

- Turn up the speed of the inline fan so more hot air is pulled out of the grow environment. Make sure to monitor the humidity when the change is made because humidity will also be pulled from the grow environment.

- Add an air conditioner to the grow environment. Placing an air conditioner outside of the grow tent pointing towards the intake vent will allow cool air to get sucked in through the intake vent and will help lower the temperature in the environment.

- Lower the grow light ballast to a lower wattage. Reducing the wattage on the ballast will reduce the heat being produced by the grow light; therefore, doing so will reduce the heat in the environment.

- If the plant has encountered heat stress, feed it seaweed kelp extract to help it recover.

LIGHT BURN

- Move the grow light up! Depending on the wattage of the grow light and the size of the environment, the grow light may need to be 24"-36" above the top of the plant canopy.

- Lower the grow light ballast to a lower wattage. The grow light will then produce less light since the ballast is dimmed to a lower wattage.

- Top the plant so it is smaller (vegetation stage only).
  LST the plant so it is away from the grow light.

Heat stress

Light burn/bleaching

Over-Watering & UNDER-WATERING

DESCRIPTION: The plant's roots need oxygen for a process called respiration. If there is too much water in the grow pot, the plant's roots cannot intake the necessary oxygen it needs. The leaves of the plant will then droop/curl down. However, the symptoms of under-watering are the same as over-watering – so do not get the two confused. The plant's leaves will also droop/curl down if it does not have enough water.

Note The plant will naturally droop/curl down after every watering. This is normal and the plant should be back to normal within 3-8 hours.

PROBLEM: Leaves are drooping/curling down on the plant. Long-term over-watering will also show yellowing of the plant's leaves.

SOLUTION(S): Over-Watering
- Make sure that the grow pot that the plant grows in has enough drainage.
- Only water the plant when the top inch of the medium is dry.

Under-Watering
- Water the plant as instructed in the Watering section of this book.

PROBLEMS

Nitrogen
DEFICIENCY

DESCRIPTION: Nitrogen is one of the main nutrients that the cannabis plant needs to grow. Nitrogen keeps the plant's leaves green and, as a result, can turn light into energy for the plant. If not enough nitrogen is given to the plant, the plant will use up nitrogen from lower leaves in order to feed the upper part of the plant.

PROBLEM: Yellowing of leaves on the lower part of the plant. The yellow leaves will become soft and eventually crispy up and fall off the plant by itself.

Note It is normal for yellowing to occur towards the final weeks of the flowering stage. This means the plant used the last of the nitrogen in the soil to produce buds. Furthermore, no action should be taken if this is your scenario.

SOLUTION(S): Feed the plant nitrogen. Increase the nutrient dose you give the plant. The plant should be fed nutrients according to the stage it is in – vegetation or flower. For example, the FoxFarm trio of nutrients has Grow Big bottle for the vegetation stage and Tiger Bloom bottle for the flower stage. The minerals included in those bottles are different since plants use up minerals differently in the vegetation and flower stages. To put it simply, if the plant is in the vegetation stage, feed it nutrients intended for the vegetation stage. If the plant is in the flower stage, feed it nutrients intended for the flower stage.

Nitrogen TOXICITY

DESCRIPTION: Nitrogen is needed for the process of photosynthesis. Although, too much nitrogen is toxic and will stunt the growth of the plant. If the plant gets nitrogen toxicity in the flowering stage, bud development will greatly suffer and the result will be airy buds instead of dense buds. Cannabis uses up more nitrogen in the vegetation stage than in the flower stage.

PROBLEM: Look out for clawing of the leaves. Clawing occurs when the tips of the leaves bend down. If not treated, those leaves will turn yellow and die. Another sign of nitrogen toxicity is dark green leaves. Dark green leaves start at the bottom of the plant and will go up as the issue gets worse.

SOLUTION(S): First, check the pH and PPM to see if they are within the ideal ranges. Nitrogen toxicity will usually happen if the pH is below 6.0 and/or the PPM is above the ideal range (PPM ideal ranges are listed in the PPM section of this book). If the pH is too low or PPM is too high, flush the plant. Decrease the nutrient dose you give the plant. Some brands of nutrients such as the FoxFarm trio line show a suggested dosage on the feeding schedule which is too high for cannabis plants. Feed the plant ½ dose or ¼ dose of what is suggested. As long as the plant is properly flushed and the pH and PPM are in the ideal ranges, the plant should recover.

Calcium
DEFICIENCY

DESCRIPTION: Calcium is a nutrient that moves slowly throughout the plant. Calcium provides structure to the plant, but also helps the plant withstand stress from heat. The plant's roots can best absorb calcium when the pH is in the 6.2-7.0 range. Calcium deficiency typically happens if using reverse osmosis water since calcium is filtered from it. Also, if using LED grow lights, the plant will likely uptake more calcium than other grow lights do due to the light's impact on photosynthesis.

PROBLEM: Spotting on the leaves that look like rust (brown spots). This problem tends to show up on the leaves directly exposed to the light. It also tends to appear on newly grown leaves. If untreated, stems will become weak and if in the flower stage, bud development will slow down.

SOLUTION(S): Feed the plant calcium. I recommend picking up a bottle CalMag and start feeding it to the plant as suggested on the bottle. Continue feeding CalMag until two weeks prior to harvest. Keep in mind that once the calcium deficiency is resolved, the leaves that were impacted with spotting will remain. Therefore, check new growth to ensure issue is resolved.

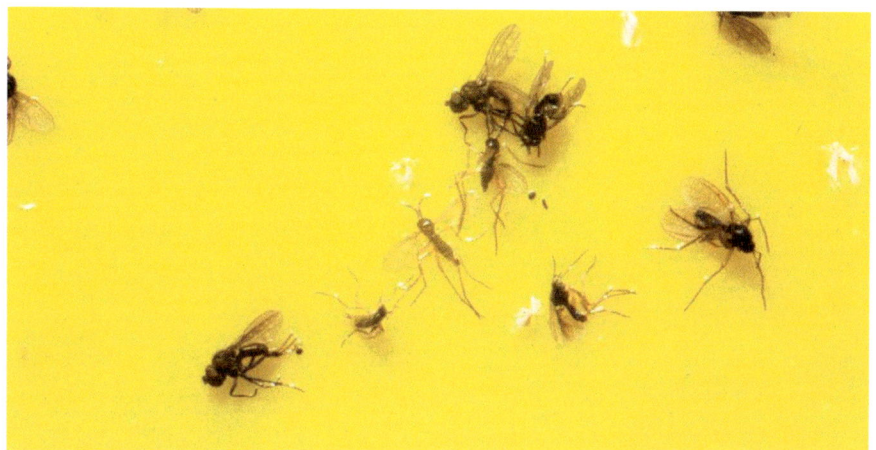

Fungus GNATS

DESCRIPTION: Fungus gnats are black or dark brown flies that commonly appear when plants are over watered. They thrive in wet conditions. Fungus gnats will show up, fly round on top of the soil, and also lay eggs in the soil. If gone untreated, the gnats will harm the plant's roots which will lead to other plant problems.

PROBLEM: Fungus gnats appear on top of the soil. They will lay eggs which hatch into larvae that look like tiny maggots. They then live in the top 2-3 inches of the soil and will eat away at the plant's roots. This will cause problems in the plant's leaves as well as slow down the growth of the plant.

SOLUTION(S): Let the top inch of the soil dry out and the fungus gnats will go away on their own. Water the plants by following the steps in the Watering section of this book. To dry out the soil faster, point a fan to blow air directly over the soil. Purchase yellow sticky traps and place by the soil. The gnats will get stuck to the yellow sticky trap and die.

Bud Rot & MOLD

DESCRIPTION: Wet, cold environments are most at risk for bud rot and mold. Bud rot and mold can only happen if the plants are in the flower stage and buds have grown on the plant. Once the buds have gotten mold on them or rotted, they can no longer be brought back to normal. Unfortunately, those buds cannot be smoked or used.

PROBLEM: White mold on the outside of the bud is the beginning stage. Once it gets worse, the buds will become dark gray or brown on the inside. You may also see fungus spores which look like dust.

SOLUTION(S): Keep humidity lower than 60% while in the flower stage. Add an oscillating fan to circulate air in the grow environment to help remove humid spots. Any part of the plant that has bud rot or mold should be cut off the plant and thrown away as soon as possible. This will help prevent other parts of the plant from getting infected.

Nutrient BURN

DESCRIPTION: The plant needs nutrients to grow; although, too much can be bad and can lead to nutrient burn. New growers often make the mistake of feeding their plants too much nutrients which results in the plant's roots taking in more nutrients than it can use. Nutrient burn can also happen with newly sprouted plants that are planted in soil with high nutrients in it. Once the plant shows sign of nutrient burn on its leaves, those leaves will not recover.

PROBLEM: Tips of the plant's leaves turn brown or yellow. If gone untreated, the problem will spread to the rest of the leaves impacted and kill them.

SOLUTION(S): Check the PPM of the runoff. Nutrient burn typically occurs if the PPM of the runoff is above the ideal range. Lower the dose of nutrients fed to the plant for the next 2-3 feedings. Make sure the correct nutrients are being fed to the plants – i.e. nutrients intended for the vegetation stage should only be fed to plants in vegetation while nutrients intended for the flower stage should only be fed to plants in flower.

PROBLEMS

Hermies & BANANAS

DESCRIPTION: Hermaphrodites (aka hermies) are cannabis plants that show signs of both male and female characteristics - the plant will produce both flowers and pollen sacs. Bananas are little yellow pollen sacs that appear on the buds in the flower stage. They typically appear when the plant is stressed from drastic changes in the environment – i.e. big temperature and/or humidity swings. Inconsistent light schedules and excessive plant deficiencies can also stress out the plant enough to cause bananas to appear. Bananas could also appear on a plant that is over-ripe and ready for harvest. Once bananas start to appear on the buds and pollinate the flowers, the plant will shift its focus and energy from producing buds to producing seeds.

PROBLEM: Both flowers and pollen sacs growing on the plant and/or yellow bananas growing on the buds.

SOLUTION(S): If the plant is a hermie, the plant can still be grown and harvested as normal even though that plant will have smaller buds and seeds within the buds. Most growers will kill the plant instead. If bananas appear of the plant, some growers will use tweezers or something similar to pluck the bananas from the buds. This can be a tedious job as it is normal for 5-10 or even more bananas to appear on the plant on a daily basis. If bananas start early in flower, most growers will kill the plant. If bananas start late in flower stage, growers will typically finish growing the plant. If the plant is within a week or two of harvest, then harvest the plant.

Phosphorus
DEFICIENCY

DESCRIPTION: Phosphorus aids in root growth and influences the vigor of the plant. Much of the energy that the plant receives from the sunlight is later stored mostly as phosphorus. Phosphorus is used in order to perform photosynthesis and it also enhances bud development.

PROBLEM: Brown spots on leaves on the lower part of the plant. Leaves may also turn yellow and curl.

SOLUTION(S): This deficiency is often seen in weeks 3, 4, and 5 of the flower stage since cannabis uses a high amount of phosphorus during these weeks. Growers will also encounter phosphorus deficiency if the pH is out of the ideal range. Check the pH and adjust to the ideal range if necessary. If the plant is in the flower stage, a PK booster can be used to increase phosphorus levels. A PK booster is an additive for plants that consists of phosphorus and potassium.

Potassium
DEFICIENCY

DESCRIPTION: Potassium plays a key role in stimulating early growth. It also promotes disease resistance and improves the efficiency of water use. Under optimal potassium levels, cell walls grow strong. In turn, the cell walls help to deflect pathogens and reduce the plant's susceptibility to powdery mildew and similar infections.

PROBLEM: Brown edges on leaves that sometimes have yellow margins. The tips of the leaves curl as the edges turn brown. This deficiency is often confused with nutrient burn and light burn.

SOLUTION(S): Similar to a phosphorus deficiency, a potassium deficiency is often seen in weeks 3, 4, and 5 of the flower stage since cannabis uses a high amount of potassium during these weeks. Growers will also encounter potassium deficiency if the pH is out of the ideal range. Check the pH and adjust to the ideal range. If the plant is in the flower stage, a PK booster can be used to increase potassium levels. A PK booster is an additive for plants that consists of phosphorus and potassium.

EPILOGUE

Thank you so much for reading my book on how to grow cannabis. I hope this information helped you become more knowledgeable on the grow process resulting in successfully completing the process. Grow techniques frequently change. These changes make the process easier resulting in higher quality and bigger yields. For the most up-to-date information on growing cannabis, visit my website at www.MrGrowIt.com. I'm always updating the site with the newest information and videos.

Also, I would love to hear from you! The most rewarding aspect of writing this book is when my readers reach out to me. Follow me on YouTube, Facebook, Instagram, and Twitter @MrGrowIt for grow articles, videos, pictures, and updated information.

Happy growing,
-Mr. Grow It

GLOSSARY

▶ **ADJUSTABLE LIGHT RATCHETS**
Designed for indoor gardening grow light fixtures & reflectors. These user-friendly hangers are easy to adjust and the length can be changed regularly as the plants grow.

▶ **AUTOFLOWER PLANT**
A plant that automatically switches from vegetative growth to the flowering stage with age, as opposed to the ratio of light to dark hours required with photoperiod dependent strains.

▶ **BALLAST**
Regulates the current to a high intensity discharge (HID) light and provides sufficient voltage to start the light.

▶ **BANANAS**
Exposed male pollen sacs (stamen) that begin growing from a female plant that has been exposed to stress.

▶ **BUD ROT**
A plant disease or symptom of disease involving decay of the buds.

▶ **BURPING**
Opening the air tight container where cannabis is being stored for short periods of time allowing any extra moisture to escape that may be caused from any sweating of the cannabis buds during the curing process.

▶ **CANNABINOIDS**
A group of closely related compounds that include cannabinol and the active constituents of cannabis.

▶ **CBN**
Cannabinol (CBN) is a non-psychoactive cannabinoid found only in trace amounts in cannabis.

▶ **CANOPY**
The upper layer of a plant or group of plants.

GLOSSARY

▸ **CARBON DIOXIDE**
A colorless, odorless gas produced by burning carbon, organic compounds, and by respiration. It is naturally present in air (about 0.03 percent) and is absorbed by plants during photosynthesis.

▸ **CHLOROPHYLL**
A green pigment, present in all green plants, responsible for the absorption of light to provide energy for photosynthesis.

▸ **CLAWING**
When the tips of the leaves of a cannabis plant bend down to appear as claws due to the plant uptaking too much nitrogen.

▸ **COLA**
A cluster of buds that grow tightly together.

▸ **CUBIC FEET PER MINUTE (CFM)**
A unit of volumetric flow.

▸ **CURING**
The method of preserving cannabis.

▸ **DARK PERIOD**
The period considered to be critical in the responses of plants to changes in day length. It is believed that such responses, which include the onset of flowering, are determined by the length of the period of darkness that occurs between two periods of light.

▸ **DIODES**
A semiconductor device with two terminals, typically allowing the flow of current in one direction only. Diodes are used in LED lighting fixtures.

▸ **DRY TRIM**
Plant that is trimmed after the plant has completed the drying process.

▸ **EXHAUST VENT**
An opening that allows air to pass out of a confined space.

▸ **FLOWER STAGE**
The phase when the cannabis plants produce their flower sets.

GLOSSARY

▶ **FLUSHING**
Washing out the growing medium that a plant is in by a sudden rush of water.

▶ **FOXTAILING**
When buds start to form on top of each other to look like little towers.

▶ **GROW ENVIRONMENT**
The surroundings that the cannabis plants are grown in.

▶ **GROW POT**
A container in which flowers and other plants are cultivated and displayed.

▶ **GROW TENT**
A portable, reusable grow room made of a sturdy canvas exterior and will usually have reflective interior material to increase light reflection onto plants.

▶ **GROWING MEDIUM**
A substance through which plant roots grow and extract water and nutrients.

▶ **HARD WATER**
Water with a high amount of minerals.

▶ **HEAT STRESS**
Where temperatures are hot enough for sufficient time that they cause irreversible damage to plant function or development.

▶ **HERMAPHRODITE**
An organism that has reproductive organs normally associated with both male and female sexes.

▶ **HIGH INTENSITY DISCHARGE (HID)**
A family of gas-discharge arc lamps which create light by sending an electrical discharge between two electrodes and through a plasma, or ionized gas.

▶ **HIGH PRESSURE SODIUM (HPS)**
A gas-discharge lamp that uses sodium in an excited state to produce light at a characteristic wavelength near 589 nm.

GLOSSARY

▶ **HOT SPOT**
A small area or region with a relatively hot temperature in comparison to its surroundings.

▶ **HUMID POCKETS**
A small area or region with a high humidity in comparison to its surroundings.

▶ **INTAKE VENT**
An opening that allows air to pass into a confined space.

▶ **LIGHT BLEACHING**
Whitening of the plant due to exposure of excessive light.

▶ **LIGHT CYCLE**
Refers to the cycle of light and darkness in which a plant receives.

▶ **LIGHT-EMITTING DIODE (LED)**
A semiconductor device that emits visible light when an electric current passes through it.

▶ **METAL HALIDE (MH)**
An electrical lamp that produces light by an electric arc through a gaseous mixture of vaporized mercury and metal halides.

▶ **MYLAR**
A form of polyester resin used to make heat-resistant plastic films and sheets.

▶ **NODE**
The area of a plant's stem from which the leaves grow.

▶ **NPK RATIO**
N-P-K refers to the ratio of important elements in a fertilizer or soil amendment. N stands for nitrogen, which is responsible for strong stem and foliage growth. P is for phosphorus, which aids in healthy root growth and flower and seed production. K stands for potassium, which is responsible for improving overall health and disease resistance.

▶ **NUTRIENT LOCKOUT**
A situation in which the roots of the plants are unable to take up the nutrients present, and additional fertilizer applications will not help.

GLOSSARY

▶ **PARTS PER MILLION (PPM)**
A unit of measurement that measures the amount of dissolved solids in a solution in terms of a ratio between the number of parts of solids to a million parts of total volume.

▶ **PHOTOPERIOD PLANT**
A plant that will not flower until the light cycle is changed so it receives 12 hours of darkness daily.

▶ **PHOTOSYNTHESIS**
The process by which green plants and some other organisms use sunlight to synthesize foods from carbon dioxide and water. Photosynthesis in plants generally involves the green pigment chlorophyll and generates oxygen as a byproduct.

▶ **PISTILS**
The female organs of a flower comprising of the stigma, style, and ovary.

▶ **PK BOOSTER**
Nutrient supplements for flowering plants that are specifically designed to be used during middle and late stages of flowering periods.

▶ **POLLEN SACS**
The structure in a plant in which pollen is produced.

▶ **PRUNING**
Trimming a plant by cutting away dead or overgrown branches or stems, especially to increase fruitfulness and growth.

▶ **RESPIRATION**
A process in living organisms involving the production of energy, typically with the intake of oxygen and the release of carbon dioxide from the oxidation of complex organic substances.

▶ **REVERSE OSMOSIS (RO)**
A water purification technology that remove ions, molecules, and larger particles from the water.

▶ **RUNOFF**
The water that comes out from the bottom of the grow pot.

▶ **SPROUT**
A shoot of a plant that grows, springs up, or comes forth from a growing medium.

GLOSSARY

▶ **STIPULES**
A small leaf-like appendage to a leaf, typically borne in pairs at the base of the leaf stalk.

▶ **STRAIN**
Either pure or hybrid varieties of the cannabis genus of plants that encompasses the species sativa, indica and ruderalis.

▶ **TAP ROOT**
A straight tapering root growing vertically downward and forming the center from which subsidiary rootlets spring.

▶ **THC**
Tetrahydrocannabinol (THC) is a compound that is the physiologically active component in cannabis.

▶ **TOPPING**
Cutting off the top of a stem.

▶ **TRANSPLANT SHOCK**
A term that refers to a number of stresses occurring in recently transplanted plants.

▶ **TRANSPLANTING**
Replanting (a plant) in another place.

▶ **TRICHOMES**
A small hair or other outgrowth from the epidermis of a plant, typically unicellular and glandular.

▶ **TRIMMING**
Removing plant leaves by cutting them off.

▶ **VEGETATION STAGE**
The phase of plant growth that occurs after germination and before flowering, during which the plant develops the majority of its foliage and truly flourishes.

▶ **WET TRIM**
A plant is trimmed before the plant is dry.

▶ **WIND BURN**
A strong wind that whips around the plants and dries out parts of the plants.

▶ **YIELD**
The full amount of an agricultural or industrial product.

Made in United States
Orlando, FL
28 October 2021